Key Issues for Education Researchers

Education Studies: Key Issues

In the last fifteen years or so Education Studies has developed rapidly as a distinctive subject in its own right. Beginning initially at undergraduate level, this expansion is now also taking place at masters level and is characterised by an increasingly analytical approach to the study of education. As education studies programmes have developed there has emerged a number of discrete study areas that require indepth texts to support student learning.

'Introduction to Education Studies: Second Edition' is the core text in this series and gives students an important grounding in the study of education. It provides an overview of the subject and introduces the reader to fundamental theories and debates in the field. The series, 'Key Issues in Education Studies,' has evolved from this core text and, using the same critical approach, each volume outlines a significant area of study within the education studies field. All of the books have been written by experts in their area and provide the detail and depth required by students as they progress further in the subject.

Taken as a whole, this series provides a comprehensive set of texts for the student of education. Whilst of particular value to students of Education Studies, the series will also be instructive for those studying related areas such as Childhood Studies and Special Needs, as well as being of interest to students on initial teacher training courses and practitioners working in education.

We hope that this series provides you, the reader, with plentiful opportunities to explore further this exciting and significant area of study and we wish you well in your endeavours.

Steve Bartlett and Diana Burton

Key Issues for Education Researchers

Diana Burton and Steve Bartlett

Los Angeles | London | New Delhi
Singapore | Washington DC

First published 2009

SAGE Publications Ltd
1 Oliver's Yard
55 City Road
London EC1Y 1SP

SAGE Publications Inc.
2455 Teller Road
Thousand Oaks, California 91320

SAGE Publications India Pvt Ltd
B 1/I 1 Mohan Cooperative Industrial Area
Mathura Road
New Delhi 110 044

SAGE Publications Asia-Pacific Pte Ltd
33 Pekin Street #02-01
Far East Square
Singapore 048763

Library of Congress Control Number: 2008940127

British Library Cataloguing in Publication data

A catalogue record for this book is available from the British Library

ISBN 978-1-84787-357-6
ISBN 978-1-84787-358-3 (pbk)

Typeset by C&M Digitals (P) Ltd, Chennai, India
Printed and bound in Great Britain by the MPG Books Group
Printed on paper from sustainable resources

Contents

Introduction: The purpose and structure of this text

Who is this book for?

We have written this book for those setting out on their early research experiences. It is specifically aimed at students of Education Studies and related subjects, those returning to the study of education as part of their professional development, and also students embarking on research at Masters level. Readers of our other research text, *Practitioner Research for Teachers* (Burton and Bartlett, 2005), will recognise many of the topics and ideas presented in this new book built upon within a broader frame of reference for students of education in addition to practising professionals. As such, it includes practical examples of research approaches from a wider range of educational settings. Readers of our core text, *Introduction to Education Studies* (Bartlett and Burton, 2007) will see the ideas addressed in the research chapter of that book developed and exemplified in far greater detail to provide a text which effectively shows you how to design, develop, conduct, evaluate and write up your research.

Studying in higher education requires the student to be able to critically appraise and use current research within their field. In order to do this effectively a good knowledge and understanding of the research process is required. Also, at some point in most undergraduate programmes and in all masters courses it will be expected that students should conduct research themselves in their relevant subject area.

This research can be on a variety of scales and take on many different forms. On many occasions you will have to collect evidence as part of your learning. The amount required will vary greatly depending on the purpose for which it is intended. Thus you may be expected to find out the opinions of other students on a particular issue, visit a site of education or training to gather some basic data on the services offered, or trawl government websites as part of an analysis of national policy. These are very different types of evidence collected in a variety of ways and they will be used differently within each module or programme of study. Many undergraduate students, for example, will have to collect evidence from a range of sources as part of a work-based learning module. Masters students will often have to conduct professional evaluations of different aspects of their work. In both instances, students need to employ their skills of collecting and analysing data in an appropriate manner.

It is important to understand the strengths and limitations of the data that you are using. These will determine how you are able to use the information to support or counter different arguments. As you progress through your programmes you will also, inevitably, become involved in conducting larger pieces of research when you have to complete undergraduate and Masters dissertations.

What does this book do?

In this book we aim to introduce you to the the nature of research and how it can be conducted. Hopefully this will enable you to be able to critique existing research in a constructive way and also begin to develop your own data collection and analytical skills. We use a wide range of practical examples of research conducted by undergraduate and postgraduate researchers throughout. For example, there are small pieces of research conducted by students as part of undergraduate modules; research and evaluation carried out by professionals as part of their practice; research conducted for Masters and PhD theses; and also some projects conducted by university researchers. The purpose of such a wide range of examples is to broaden your horizons about the scope and levels of research projects. We have recommended reading to encourage you to develop your knowledge and understanding further and student activities to help you develop the skills needed to conduct research.

We begin by looking at what the term 'research' means and why we need to do it. In this section we not only hope to dispel some of the fear and mystique surrounding this term but also to show that while we can all conduct research, the purpose must always be to do it in the most relevant way and to the highest quality that we possibly can. Chapter 1 goes on to look at some of the recent movements in the field of education research and also some of their critiques. In Chapter 2 we then consider the different positions that can be taken on research and the paradigms within which research positions are framed. The positioning of researchers is very significant, as will be made clear, as this influences the areas they will consider important enough to investigate and the types of research they will value over others. At this point we examine ethical positions within the research process in Chapter 3. Alongside the positioning of the researcher, his or her ethical values will significantly influence the whole research process. In Chapter 4 we look at the research process and how to get started on your research project. This chapter will enable you to begin to plan the whole process.

Before you begin your own data collection it is important that you consider what has already been done and written in your chosen area. This is vital in terms of developing a deeper understanding of the focus of your research. It will also enable you to place your own contribution in the existing field. Chapter 5 explains how to carry out and write a literature review. We then go on in Chapter 6 to look at case study research as this is a common approach used by researchers in education, particularly when conducting small-scale research. We also consider the possibility of experiments, a strategy borrowed and adapted from the natural sciences.

The following chapters (7 to 10) look at a range of methods that may be used to collect data in your research project. Within these chapters we discuss questionnaires, interviews, observation, diaries, logs and biographies, and the use of existing data in the form of written and visual material. In the final chapter we discuss the writing up of your research project and offer structured guidance. This is a very important, though often neglected, part of the research process and can be particularly significant when the research is part of an academic programme and thus will be submitted as a project or thesis.

By the time you reach the end of the book and have completed the student activities set you will have already embarked on your career as a researcher. A career that we hope will be long and exciting.

1

The development of education research

This chapter discusses the meaning of the term 'research' and shows how it forms part of our daily lives. The characteristics of formal research are outlined and different typologies of research identified. Significant movements in research in education will be discussed, including school effectiveness, school improvement, action and practitioner approaches to education research.

What is research?

When we think of research it may seem daunting because it is generally felt to be associated with complex methods and to have a mystique that precludes amateurs. However, we are all used to doing research or gathering data in many ways on a daily basis. The methods we typically use to find things out include observing situations or particular events, watching television, asking different people, looking things up in books, or surfing the web. All of this normal activity constitutes data collection. We do it to make sense of the world in which we operate. As new information becomes available to us in our daily lives we are constantly checking, modifying, refining and developing what we know. In the world of education teachers, lecturers, students and pupils are constantly 'interpreting' what is going on around them in the educational environments of their classroom, lecture theatre, workshop and laboratory. They will carefully listen, observe, and wait for responses to specific actions.

It is apparent that the skills of the researcher are very significant and that these skills improve with practice. Our personal research methods are in permanent use. We are aware that information gathered may vary and even conflict so we become skilled at analysing and evaluating data, making decisions as to its validity or truthfulness. We may expect to hear rather different accounts, for instance, of a local football match when we ask the players from the two teams, their supporting families and friends, and even the referee. All of these different accounts, though, are useful in developing our global understanding of the event. Consider how a teacher may carefully question several pupils to find out what happened in a particular incident. An experienced teacher is likely to recognise the subtle differences that would result in the information gathered when pupils are questioned individually, in pairs, or in groups. That teacher will alter their questioning accordingly.

We receive information daily from a wide range of sources. Some of this is even portrayed as research findings. In a typical evening's television viewing, for example, information about political conflict and war, economic developments, garden design, possible holiday destinations, the benefits of particular washing powders, may be presented to us. We evaluate and store or disregard all the information presented to us. Different types of research results are presented to help inform our opinions and make decisions about, for example, smoking or not smoking, using or not using drugs and alcohol, or which trainers to buy. We accept some data more readily than others and though we may enjoy certain adverts, such as for a particular deodorant, we will remain sceptical of its claims for increasing our sexual magnetism. Presentation impacts differently on people and is a major concern of the advertiser. This is worth remembering when we begin to look at how academic or formal research is presented. Throughout this book we suggest that you must consider numerous ways of looking at things and should maintain a robustly critical approach to all research findings.

 Student Activity

Understanding the power of positioning

No research into aspects of education, no matter how detailed, extensive and apparently objective, can tell the whole story. All research is positioned. Consider how your own views on an aspect of education have affected your ability to be objective in considering a particular set of research findings.

Formal research

What does the term 'research' mean when used in relation to the study of education? Blaxter et al. (2006: 5) explain that

> All types of research should be planned, cautious, systematic, and reliable ways of finding out or deepening understanding.

Definitions abound, but the use of such words as 'systematic', 'reliable' and 'cautious' is characteristic of most because, for researchers, the rigour of their approach is paramount. Evans and King point to the fundamental role of research in interpreting information and building theories.

> Research is not just about gathering information, it is also about analysing and interpreting that information and using it to make predictions or to build theories about the way the world works – or parts of it at least! (2006: 131)

Verma and Mallick (1999) suggest that research has attained a high degree of respectability and that educators, politicians, business people and others will turn to researchers when seeking information on which to base decisions. Most advanced societies have evolved a research-oriented culture, or are in the process of moving in that direction. Formal research, then, would appear to be the systematic gathering, presenting and analysing of data. Actually, some research is more systematic than others. Some research is more formalised than others. The process can appear mysterious to 'outsiders', making researchers seem special and somehow different. It is important to 'demystify' the process in the rest of this chapter since we are all players of the research game.

Academic research essentially refines the information-gathering practices of our daily living. Watching other people becomes observation, asking questions becomes interviewing. If the questions are written down you have a questionnaire. The difference is that these information-gathering practices are carried out in a more conscious manner. They become more structured, rigorous and deliberate. The findings are recorded systematically and with care. The research methods are formalised for a number of possible motives: to make them more 'scientific', to make them larger scale, to make them more authoritative, to 'prove' them, to inform action, to take them further than individual experiences. Research, however complex or formally presented, is simply a part of the process of finding out and understanding phenomena.

Purposes of research

Clough and Nutbrown (2007) explain that all social research is persuasive, purposive, positional and political and these are the reasons why it is conducted. The need to persuade someone or a group of people about something underlies all research, whether it is persuading customers to buy a particular product or persuading teachers of a particular teaching method. Research is purposive in that it attempts to produce something, such as the solution to a problem. Research is positional because it is imbued with the perspective of the researcher and the research funders and is derived from a set of circumstances where a problem was defined necessarily from a particular viewpoint or position. As Clough and Nutbrown observe

> Research which did not express a more or less distinct perspective on the world would not be research at all; it would have the status of a telephone directory where data are listed without analysis (p. 10).

Finally research is political because it seeks to make a difference within a policy context. Practitioner researchers, for instance, may seek to change the behaviour policy of a school based on research they have conducted into the efficiency of sanctions.

Types of research

We can never dissociate the motives for and context of our research from the types of research methods we employ. There are a great many types of research defined either by their context, e.g. market research, or by their approach. Verma and Mallick developed the following typology of research which highlights 'critical differences between research that is oriented to the development of theory and that is designed to deal with practical problems' (1999: 11).

- **Pure or basic research**
  Concerned with the development of theory and the discovery of fundamental facts to extend the boundaries of knowledge.
- **Applied or field research**
  The application of new knowledge to everyday problems. Though more practical it usually employs the same rigorous methodology as pure research.
- **Action research**
  Research into specific practical situations carried out by practitioners to solve clearly identified problems in order to improve them. As such it is continuous and cyclical. (Action research is discussed in more detail in the following chapter.)
- **Evaluation research**
   This is carried out to assess the effectiveness of specific projects to see if the original aims have been achieved. Many government-funded projects will allocate a proportion of their budgets for evaluation.

Hammersley (2002) suggests a distinction between what he terms *scientific* and *practical* research. The criteria of validity and relevance are important to both types of research but are given different weight and interpreted differently within each.

Hammersley further divides scientific enquiry into:

- **theoretical scientific research**
- **substantive scientific research.**

Practical research subdivides into:

- **dedicated practical research** the goal of which is to provide information to a specific group;
- **democratic practical research** that provides information for anyone interested in a particular issue;

- **contract-based practical research** where the project is commissioned to produce information on a specific issue;
- **autonomous practical research** when researchers are autonomous in how they approach an issue of interest.

Both Hammersley's and Verma and Mallick's typologies highlight the key point that there are different types of research with different purposes. Each will have particular strengths and weaknesses, and whilst these types of research are complementary to each other, 'criticism arises, in part at least, from the impossibility of satisfying, simultaneously, all the criteria by which research findings can be judged' (Hammersley, 2002: 124).

Research in education

Education, whether considered in its informal or its more formal institutionalised guises, constitutes a signficant part of society and social life so there are many academic subjects interested in it as an area of research. Historians in their studies of processes over time, for example, have looked at developments in and influences of education. Lawson and Silver (1973) examined the social history of education in England from Anglo-Saxon times up until the late 1960s. Jones (2003) analysed changes in education in Britain from 1944 to the early years of the 'New' Labour government, linking these to the wider economic, political and social developments that occurred over this period. Sociologists have also studied the part that education plays in the structure of society and the power relationships it involves. Bowles and Gintis (1976), for example, analysed how state education helps to maintain capitalism by socialising working-class pupils into accepting their position. Hargreaves (1967) looked at how the labelling and setting processes that took place in schools helped to reinforce social inequality. Psychology helps explain aspects of individual development, thus the learning theories of psychologists such as Piaget (1932, 1952) and Vygotsky (1978) are clearly educationally based. Economists also have an interest in the development of the workforce as a factor of production. For the economist, education is a product to be demanded and supplied and so it is studied as part of market behaviour. Economists will compare, for instance, the supply of education as a public good and conversely via the free market. These examples can perhaps be characterised as coming from the more traditionally academic areas of study. It is also clear that these areas of study, which may be termed the social sciences, are closely related to each other and overlap. This type of research into education is often termed *education research*.

Though not totally separate from academic study there are some researchers who feel actively involved in the education process itself. Indeed they may be educational professionals themselves and their research is usually related to teaching and learning and shows a desire for social improvement and the promotion of social justice. This research is more *applied*, with a focus on improving educational experiences, opportunities and achievement. As such it can be very attractive to politicians wishing to promote populist policies – the raising of standards, for example. Research that has an ultimate concern with changing education itself, emanating from a desire to improve things that is conducted by those whose prime area of interest is education rather than a traditional academic discipline, and who often have a professional interest in the area, is frequently called *educational research*. For instance, Elliott (2006) contrasts educational research which he sees as shaped by a pragmatic theory of knowledge with *research on education* that he suggests is shaped by a 'spectator' theory. Pring (2004) draws a distinction between what he sees as research that is 'embedded in the social sciences which may well be relevant to education and that which arises from educational concerns and which draws upon, but is not to be reduced to, the knowledge which has accumulated within those sciences (p. 9).

Thus there are different types of research stemming from different purposes and traditions that may in a rather confusing way be termed 'education' or 'educational research'. These are both about education, but have different purposes.

> **Research which seeks to explain or comment upon educational phenomena and processes is known as** *education research*.
>
> **Research which seeks to change or improve educational experiences is known as** *educational research*.

A crisis in educational research

In the past two decades there have been fierce debates about the nature and value of educational research. In the Teacher Training Agency Annual Lecture of 1996, David Hargreaves, an influential UK educationalist, highlighted what he saw as the failure of educational research to serve those working in education. Hargreaves suggested that educational research at that time was poor value for money and that it inadequately served the teaching profession. He called for the setting up of a National Education Research Forum 'which would shape the agenda of educational research and its policy implications and applications' (1996: 6). He also suggested that funding should be redirected away from academic researchers to agencies committed to evidence-based practice and to fund teachers as researcher-practitioners. In this way teaching would become an evidence-based profession. This speech, whilst promoting heated debate amongst both academics and professionals concerned with education, was a forerunner of the TTA policy that promoted practitioner research (TTA, 1996).

Both the Tooley Report (Tooley and Darby, 1998) funded by OfSTED, and the Hillage Report (Hillage et al., 1998) funded by the DfES, also raised questions concerning the quality and usefulness of educational research. Hammersley (2002) and Elliott (2001) argued that these criticisms, Hargreaves' in particular, all took a rather simplistic view of how research was able to inform practice. They made the assumption that research can show definite cause and effect relationships and will point to clear routes for action. However, the reality is far more complex and thus we should treat the whole research process as problematic by taking a more interpretivist approach to educational research.

If, as Hammersley (2002) and others would argue, there are different forms of research that are carried out for different purposes, it could be claimed that their outcomes should be evaluated differently because they offer complementary strengths and weaknesses. To conclude, Whitty (2006) states that there is a need to promote all types of education research regardless of its utility for policy makers. He goes on to suggest that the education research community should ensure that appropriate quality criteria are developed for all approaches. There is, in our view, every reason and every need to assign a parity of status to 'professional' and 'academic' research. We will now consider several different movements in research in education.

The development of action research

The development of action research is often attributed to the work of Kurt Lewin (1946) who was seeking ways of increasing productivity in industry by involving a larger proportion of the workforce in decision making. He also saw what was to be termed the 'action research approach' as a way of tackling many of the social problems that were obvious in the wake of the Second World War. He developed a spiral of action that involved fact finding, planning and execution. This act of professionals conducting research in order to solve professional problems could be easily applied to many areas, with education being a prime example.

The action research 'movement' in education in Britain was greatly influenced by the work of Lawrence Stenhouse at the Schools' Council (1967–72), who believed in the professional desire of teachers to improve education for their pupils and so benefit society. Action research grew, in part, out of a disillusionment with traditional forms of education research that were conducted by the universities during the 1960s and 1970s.

Action research was seen as a new approach to research carried out by professionals. It was thus rooted in practice and moved away from the traditional academic approach based upon the major research paradigms. McNiff (1988) spoke of a desire to create a study of education that was grounded in practice and developed by all those involved. This process needed to be rigorous and critical if it was to create effective change. Thus injunctions to become more critical meant far more than simply evaluating practice for the many proponents of action research (Carr and Kemmis, 1986). The development of critical theory was seen as a questioning of the whole purpose and techniques employed by teachers. It involved asking fundamental questions about why things were done in a certain way and why other processes were not used. This would then encourage further research, experimentation and, ultimately, change. There would be a linking of theory and practice alongside the development of research for action.

 Student Activity

Bearing in mind the earlier explanation of the different types of research, would you say that this research approach identified above is *education research* or *educational research*?

Defining action research

According to Elliott, a lifelong proponent, action research is 'the study of a social situation with a view to improving the quality of action within it' (1991: 69), and 'theorising from the standpoint of action in order to act with "understanding" of the practical situation' (2003). Altrichter et al. (1993) suggest that action research starts from practical questions that fit in with the working conditions of practitioners. Methods of data collection are tailored to suit the circumstances. Each research project is designed for a specific set of circumstances and so is unique.

These definitions indicate that action research starts with a problem, issue or set of questions arising out of professional concerns. Initial research is carried out to collect data that will clarify the situation. A plan of action is devised in the light of this evidence. This is put into place and the effects carefully monitored. This is likely to lead to further refined questions and so further developments which will, in turn, be implemented and researched. However, what is critical for Elliott (2003) is that the action part of improving practice is an integral part of the teacher's construction of new knowledge and understanding of the problem. The action research process has frequently been shown in diagrammatic form as some form of developmental spiral.

The nature of this form of research means that it is carried out in the practitioner's own place of work and so the case study approach is the most common, with the researcher using a variety of methods to examine the particular issue. *Reflexivity* is an important aspect of action research and it is expected that this will be heightened as researchers develop their skills.

Increased validity is aimed at through a rigorous approach to the research coupled with triangulation and openness at all stages of the process. Though it is not possible to generalise from the findings of such small-scale research, its strength, according to Bassey (1990), lies in its relatability to similar situations. Validity is also strengthened as communities of researchers in schools examine and discuss each other's findings, an activity described by Elliott (1993) as 'discoursive consciousness'. This process would involve others and develop a wider understanding of the nature of education as part of the social

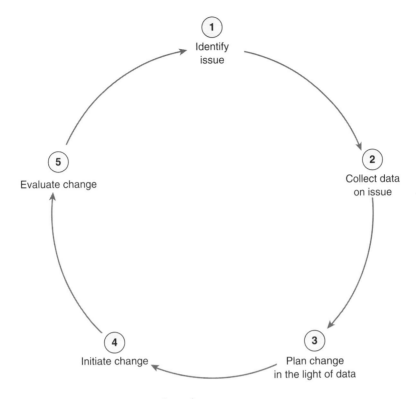

Figure 1.1   A simple action research cycle

democratic process. Kemmis and Wilkinson (1998) also stress the participatory nature of action research. They see action research itself as a social and educational process that is part of the development of a professional community.

Criticisms of action research

The use of diagrams showing action research as a continuous process of development has been criticised as inadvertently promoting a rigid approach to research (Carter and Halsall, 1998). Dadds, for instance, realised that 'the tidy action research cycle was never that tidy in the practices of research' (Dadds and Hart, 2001: 7). Diagrams that indicate stages in a research cycle may encourage the view that these show the 'correct' order in which to conduct action research. This may then create problems when any new researcher finds that they are deviating from these proscribed stages. In fairness, many of those who designed action research diagrams only intended them to be used as guides that were not proscriptive in any way. Thus McNiff (2002) explains how the action research process can actually take many turns.

The action research approach has also been accused of assuming that research begins with what might appear as a management issue – a premise that something is wrong that needs to be fixed or made better. However, many teachers may be interested, initially, in developing a broader understanding of the learning process rather than investigating problems. For these reasons Hopkins (2008) prefers to use the phrase 'classroom research by teachers' and Carter and Halsall (1998) 'teacher research' rather than action research.

Action research at the beginning of the twenty-first century

There have always been different interpretations of what action research actually involves (Bryant, 1996). For many of its proponents in the late 1970s and early 1980s it provided a whole philosophy of the future development of education through 'self-critical communities of researchers including teachers, students, parents, educational administrators and others' (Carr and Kemmis, 1986: 211).

An evangelical approach to action research that sees it as a quest for personal and professional fulfilment can still be seen in the work of many educationalists (see McNiff, 2002). However, for others it remained at the level of problem solving for teachers (see Baumfield et al., 2008, for an example of this). They were not concerned to develop a new educational science nor did they take a critical stance on the basic values and actions in their practice.

School effectiveness and school improvement research

The adoption and development of managerialist strategies in the 1980s, with their aim of increasing efficiency by improving results and reducing costs, led to a growth of interest in what became known as school effectiveness research. As its title implies, this approach sought, by using quantitative analysis, to identify what led to the creation of effective schools. Perhaps the first significant study in Britain using this approach that caught the public imagination was *Fifteen Thousand Hours* by Rutter et al. (1979). Using statistical techniques comparisons of schools were made which identified the factors that set more successful schools apart from the less successful. Over the years the lists of these characteristics have been added to and refined by a number of studies (see Creemers, 1994; Reynolds, 1994; Sammons et al., 1995; Teddlie and Reynolds, 2000). These lists tend to be very similar, usually citing strong and effective leadership, high expectations of pupil achievement and behaviour, an orderly atmosphere with an emphasis on learning, the monitoring of pupil progress, and clear enforced discipline with a positive reinforcement of success.

However, various criticisms have been levelled at school effectiveness research (see Carter, 1998; Elliott, 1998; Willmott, 1999; Thrupp, 2001). The data collected were statistical and there were issues concerning accuracy of measurement. Indeed it was questionable as to whether an agreed definition could even be arrived at for many of the factors, such as 'an orderly atmosphere' or 'effective leadership'. The term 'effective' is itself value laden when applied to education. There are different opinions as to what constitutes an effective school, or effective teaching. Many felt that this research considered effectiveness from a managerial perspective only. It became tied to measurable outcomes and these were then taken as important outcomes of education. Thus exam results and truancy figures may be used to judge effectiveness but not the happiness of pupils or the job satisfaction of the teachers. However, many of the factors linked to effective schools by this research were not startling in themselves and were already regarded as important issues in schools. The difficulty for schools was to actually develop the traits that were seen as linked to effectiveness. So, whilst identifying and developing lists of what could be seen as almost common-sense factors linked to school effectiveness, this research gave no indication of how schools could work towards these. As this research was carried out by 'outside' researchers rather than teachers, the findings often appeared as just another presentation of management ideology being passed down from above. The result was that they were often treated with cynicism by those working in schools.

This disillusionment with the positivist approach of school effectiveness research and its associated ideology was countered by the development of the 'school improvement movement'. This has the individual school at its core and through a research approach seeks to develop and implement strategies that will lead to improvement. It encourages a more eclectic approach to data collection and can therefore take a less restricted view of what is meant by school improvement. School improvement research sees each school as a community and recognises the significance of those with a 'stake' in the findings being involved in the research (see Hopkins, 2008, also Hopkins and Harris, 2000).

 Student Activity

Personal research skills

Think of something you have needed to arrange, perhaps a visit somewhere, a holiday, or a present for someone.

1. What research did you need to do beforehand?
2. List the particular data collection methods you used and the sources you accessed.
3. Note down how you triangulated your data, e.g. cross-checking between information on the internet and that received by word of mouth.
4. How did you consider the accuracy of the data you gathered?

Practitioner research

Whilst the notion of teachers as researchers seemed increasingly out of place in the Conservative administrations from 1979 until 1997, the climate changed somewhat under 'New Labour'. Research continued to be focused on school improvement perspectives but talk of partnerships in education with all stake-holders working together to raise standards became the norm. There was also a re-examination of the professional nature of teaching. The Labour government appeared to recognise the importance of teachers developing their classroom skills and how this might be achieved through reflective practice.

Perhaps as a result of the strong social democratic and ideological views linked to action research that fell out of favour and were heavily criticised in the 1980s and early 90s, the term 'practitioner research' came to be more widely used. The field of 'practitioner research' involves a wide variety of pro-fessional and community contexts such as health care, social work, police work and schooling. These contexts create differences in the approaches prac-titioners use but a shared characteristic of each is 'a central commitment to the study of one's own professional practice by the researcher himself of her-self, with a view to improving that practice for the benefit of others' (Dadds and Hart, 2001: 7). Thus practitioner research in education can be seen as any research carried out by teachers and other education professionals, such as teacher trainers, educational advisors, and education social workers, into aspects of their work.

This research can be carried out for a variety of reasons and can take many forms. It may be conducted as part of a credit-bearing course at graduate or post-graduate level. It may be carried out as part of a curricular/performance evaluation involving a team of teachers. It may be classroom focused on an issue of particular interest or concern to a teacher. It may be the case that car-rying out a small-scale piece of research has been identified as a useful part of professional development and the research may also be seen to be in the interests of the whole school.

Thus practitioner research can be initiated for a number of reasons – such as a desire to learn more about teaching and learning, or to return to more formal academic study and gain higher qualifications, or to pursue practical solutions through the evaluation of practice. From this broad set of motives we can see that practitioner research needs to embrace a whole host of approaches.

Invariably there are significant philosophical questions of purpose that lie behind research that can never be totally ignored. Thus, when research-ing into the developing of literacy and numeracy skills in pupils, questions will arise as to the identification and measurement of these skills and also the worth we place upon them. This in turn is likely to lead to at least some reflection of the basic purposes of schooling and education. The research process helps to remind us of the sets of beliefs and values upon which education is based. Whilst the encouragement of practitioner researchers is to be welcomed it is important that this encompasses a broad approach to education and its role in society.

Conclusion

In this chapter we have looked at what is meant by the term 'research' and how this applies to the field of education. Since education is such an extensive area of study there are many types of research activity within it. We have examined a number of the significant research movements of recent years to illustrate this. In Chapter 2 we go on to examine the different positionings of researchers more closely.

Recommended Reading

Baumfield, V., Hall, E. and Wall, K. (2008) *Action Research in the Classroom*. London: Sage. Though this book does not have much discussion on the nature of action research it is full of ideas and examples of how to conduct research in the classroom. As such it is a useful text for the inexperienced researcher.

Hammersley, M. (ed.) (2002) *Educational Research and Evidence-based Practice*. London: Sage and the Open University Press. This is a collection of readings on the nature of educational research. By reading it right through you will be able to follow the debates of the 1980s, 1990s and the first decade of the new millenium.

McNiff, J. with Whitehead, J. (2002) *Action Research: Principles and Practice* (second edition). London: RoutledgeFalmer. This text discusses the principles and practices of action research and provides a useful analysis of the theoretical underpinnings and how they may be applied. Case studies are used to illustrate the part played by theory and reflection.

Whitty, G. (2002) *Making Sense of Education Policy*. London: Paul Chapman. This book considers education policy throughout the 1990s. It outlines curriculum innovation, teacher professionalism and school improvement. Whitty also evaluates Labour's education policy in terms of its fostering of social justice and inclusion. Though challenging, this is an interesting book for those working in education who are seeking a political overview.

2

Research paradigms and social perspectives

This chapter will outline the major research paradigms. It will consider positivist and interpretive approaches and how these have been significant in shaping research practice in the social sciences. Issues of what counts as data and levels of validity will be discussed here. Examples of research in education will be used to show the significance of and differences between quantitative and qualitative approaches to data collection. The chapter will also emphasise the importance of possessing a working knowledge of these paradigms when carrying out and evaluating research.

The positioning of the researcher

Each one of us has developed as an individual. We have a history that has seen us grow up in particular neighbourhoods with people who are close to us, we have been through school and many of us may have experiences of higher education and into employment. Certain things in our lives will have had a significant effect upon who we are now. Particular events shape us, sometimes single events and sometimes these take place over a period of time. These may be very personal, such as the death of someone very close to us or the birth of a child. Some may be significant to many people as well as ourselves, such as periods of mass unemployment, the outbreak of conflict and war, the celebration of a royal wedding. We also interpret events that we read about or learn about through the media in the light of our experiences which help to actively shape our views.

It is useful to look at political life as an example to see how individuals take different political positions. There are three main political parties in

English politics who occupy the House of Commons; Labour, Conservative and Liberal Democrat. Whilst there are differences in beliefs between the three and they each have their own policies on education, employment, housing and so on, on many issues they actually hold quite similar views. They all deplore crimes of violence, support the raising of education standards and advocate full employment. Where they differ is their belief in how we can achieve these things. So whilst politicians are elected as members of one particular party they do have certain views in common with those from the other two parties. Within each party though there are also differences in beliefs between MPs, even though they share a common commitment to most of their party's policies. Some hold more extreme views than others on certain issues such as immigration, the treatment of juvenile offenders, the National Health Service. Sometimes these differences can lead to arguments, splits in the party and possibly a leadership crisis. The beliefs held by anyone, including MPs, are not fixed and even the strongest may evolve over time. Thus politicians have been known to change party and, more frequently, voters to change who they vote for. If we broaden this analysis of politics we can see that we are all complex individuals who have developed distinctive personalities and personal views. These constitute our particular positions which reflect our political, social and moral values.

Our individual position will influence how we do things and so how we approach research will be no different. It is worth reconsidering the point made at the beginning of the last chapter by Clough and Nutbrown (2007) that all social research is persuasive, purposive, positional and political, and these are the reasons why it is conducted. There will be certain issues that will appeal to us more than others and there will be particular types of data that we will find more meaningful. Whilst some researchers, in the same way as some politicians, will believe that their way is best and will decide to spurn any alternatives, so others whilst still preferring their own way will realise some of the strengths of the alternatives and maintain a more 'tolerant' position of different approaches.

 ## Student Activity

Positioning yourself as a researcher

Consider the following case study of one person's 'positioning' and draw up a similar outline for yourself in order to position yourself as a researcher. You must justify this in relation to your prior experiences and reading.

 Case Study

Mike, the Humanities teacher

Mike has a degree in sociology and teaches humanities to pupils aged between 11 and 16 and economics up to 'A' level. He began teaching with a liberal belief in the possibilities that comprehensive education could improve society.

Over several years Mike became increasingly sceptical as to the power of education to benefit the position of pupils from more deprived backgrounds. He continued to teach in spite of these doubts and enjoyed working with young people from all social backgrounds and abilities. He came increasingly to wonder what difference schools did make to society. The social background of the pupils seemed a more significant factor in their achievement than academic ability. Apart from a few successes the general social order of things seemed to be reproduced through education.

This led to Mike's increasing interest in how the rhetoric of education developing opportunity for all conflicted with the reality of it actually maintaining the status quo in terms of social structure. He also became interested in how, within this education system and society in general, individuals interpret their position and are able to act, adapt and survive.

Mike moved towards this critical theory standpoint with its emphasis on social power and how people interpret and adapt to this. Whilst being attracted to the work of writers such as Althusser, Bourdieu and Apple, who examine the structures of society and how these perpetuate social inequality, he was also interested in the ability of individuals to operate within these strictures. Thus he found the work of interactionists such as Becker and Goffman attractive.

He had leanings towards Marxist theory and saw himself as a structuralist, but he was not totally deterministic in that he saw how individuals were able to use their initiative and individuality. They were not totally controlled by society and had some 'agency'. Thus the concept of structuration as developed by Giddens proved very useful in helping him to interpret and understand many social situations.

He remains interested in case studies as a research strategy in education because these can embrace a range of methods, including the use of in-depth interviews which could develop understanding of individual interpretations and actions.

Ontology

Ontology is an understanding of how the world exists. Benton and Craib say that 'an ontology is the answer one would give to the question: What kind of things are there in the world?' (2001: 4). Bryman points out that the basic ontological issues are about 'whether the social world is regarded as something external to social actors or as something that people are in the process of fashioning' (2004: 3). Thus ontology is about how we see the world and our place within it. We may see it as fixed and clear, with social structures to which we all belong in our society, or we may see it as very fluid and something that is different for each of us, existing as separate individuals.

Epistemology

Epistemology is sometimes called 'the theory of knowledge' (Benton and Craib, 2001). It is about how knowledge is created and what is seen to be legitimate knowledge. Bryman (2004) suggests that a basic epistemological issue is whether or not a natural scientific approach is suitable to studying the social world. Thus some researchers suggest that the social world can be studied according to the same principles and procedures as the natural world. Others would argue that the social world is very different to the natural world and different principles of understanding need to be applied. Thus how we believe the world exists (our ontology) will be closely linked to how we see knowledge being created and suitable means of understanding it (our epistemology). Our epistemology will lead us to the suitable methods used to the study it and our understanding of the whole research process.

Understandings of how the world exists, what counts as legitimate knowledge and how we research into it will us take on to the idea of research paradigms. Paradigms constitute a coherent set of ideas and approaches which are imbued with distinctive sets of values and beliefs. In research they are often presented as polar opposites. However, just as our discussion of the intricacies of political life revealed, this very simplistic dualistic approach doesn't take into account the complex reality of research which often does not fit neatly into a single paradigm.

 Student Activity

What is reality?

Consider whether social phenomena exist as objective realities that we live among and are born into, or whether we constantly construct meanings of things that happen around us to make sense of them.

Approaches to education research

The way in which information is collected, the valuing of certain forms of data over others, the analysis and presentation of findings, are all significant parts of the research process that affects how an educational setting is portrayed. Through a discussion of research paradigms, we can consider the fundamental beliefs underpinning the research process and how these frame the ways in which we understand the world around us.

There are different ways that we can consider what is happening in schools and other educational environments. One approach involves a search to identify the key factors influencing outcomes so that they can then be applied generally. An important part of this approach is to measure performance. Thus there is particular interest here in student attainment scores, attendance figures, delinquency rates and the variables that affect these. Central to this approach is the establishment of the cause and effect relationships that operate within education. An alternative approach seeks to explain what is happening in these educational situations using the perspectives of those involved: pupils, students, teachers, lecturers, instructors and classroom assistants. The aim here is to 'understand' more fully the complexities of the educational process and the nature of teaching and learning. There is a concern with feelings and perceptions and an admission of different perspectives that render objectification or quantification redundant. These are two approaches to understanding reality and they clearly reflect alternative ideologies or views about the value and purposes of education (see Bartlett and Burton, 2007, for a discussion of ideologies). However, whilst they are different, it is also possible to see how in some ways they are complementary since important elements within each approach are of value. These different ideologies of education have corresponding alternative beliefs concerning how research is carried out. This brings us to consider research paradigms.

What are research paradigms?

This term describes models of research that reflect a general agreement on the nature of the world and how to investigate it. Within a paradigm there would be a general consensus on the research methods that are appropriate and acceptable for gathering data and also those which are not (or are at least less) acceptable. A paradigm then:

> ... is a network of coherent ideas about the nature of the world and of the functions of researchers which, adhered to by a group of researchers, conditions the patterns of their thinking and underpins their research actions. (Bassey, 1990: 41)

In the social sciences research is often divided into two major paradigms, the positivist or quantitative and the interpretivist or qualitative. These are perhaps best seen as characteristics clustering into two general groups rather than as clear extremes.

Positivist paradigm

The positivist paradigm, stemming from the enlightenment views of Comte and Spencer (Turner, 2003), developed in the nineteenth century in the wake of the apparent success of the natural, or physical, sciences in advancing our understanding of the world. People's lives had been significantly improved by scientific advances, in particular their health and living standards (see Benton and Craib, 2001).

The traditional or natural scientific approach consists of testing an hypothesis (initial idea, unproved theory) via experiments. This often involves having two identical groups, a control group to which nothing is done and all factors which could affect it (variables) are kept constant. The other group, the experimental group, is subject to some change in conditions (certain specific variables are altered in a controlled way). In this fashion, any resulting difference between the experimental and the control group is deemed to be due to the change in the variables made by the scientist in the experiment. Experiments are able to establish cause and effect relationships. Altering a particular variable has a particular, measurable effect.

Experiments in the natural sciences are said to be objective, producing findings that are unaffected by the opinions and hopes of the researcher. The outcome of the experiment, if carried out under the same conditions, will always be consistent. Thus natural science is systematic, experiments are replicable, the results are documented and knowledge of the natural world is incremental (see Yates, 2004; McNeill and Chapman, 2005). Research in the natural sciences thus has high prestige and the findings are treated with respect. Pure research in the natural sciences also became, over the years, a focus for applied research with the potential to inform future policy. Such a status was regarded as desirable by those interested in the social world and thus an interest grew in developing the social sciences.

The positivist belief is that the approach of the natural sciences could be applied to the social world. It assumes that the social world exists in the same way as does the natural world (Yates, 2004; Evans and King, 2006). Individual behaviour is influenced by various pressures, internal (such as biological and psychological pressures) and/or external (such as the norms and values held by the social groups to which we belong). As a result regular and predictable patterns of behaviour can be said to be displayed by individuals and groups in society, creating social forces in the form of both external and internalized constraints. Individuals operate within these internalized constraints and influences which derive from interaction with the wider society.

Positivists believe that the structures that create the apparent order in social life can be discovered by research. They contend that society can be investigated in the same objective way as the natural world. This approach is empirical in that it shows something exists through observations, namely, data. Going beyond theory and debate, positivist researchers attempt to show that what is being discussed in the theories actually exists because it has the status of the external and not just hypothetical. The purpose is to uncover the 'social facts' which make up our world (see the seminal work of Durkheim, 1964, 1970).

To be objective, the positivist social science researcher would ideally like to conduct experiments in the same way as the natural scientist. Some educational research is able to use this method, for instance, certain psychological experiments (see Chapter 6 for a discussion of the experimental method in educational research). However, for much social research it is not possible to create experimental and control groups and to alter variables in a controlled way. People need to be studied in their usual environment if they are to act 'naturally'. Much of the work of the Swiss psychologist Piaget was based on experiments conducted with his own children in 'laboratory' conditions which have since been criticised for their inappropriateness. There are also moral objections to treating people in certain ways, so while it might appear to be interesting to deprive babies of human affection and see how their personalities develop, it would not be ethical to do so.

In order to show relationships between variables researchers will frequently use the comparative method. This is where groups are compared and differences are noted (McNeill and Chapman, 2005). The purpose is to identify the significant variables which can explain the differences between groups. The aim ultimately is to show cause and effect relationships. This strategy is felt to be more reliable the greater the numbers used in the comparison. For positivists size does matter. Also important is the sample's representativeness of the whole population. The findings take on greater significance when the data set is larger and can be categorised and compared in a number of ways. It is important that you as the researcher maintain an objective standpoint and keep any personal 'contamination' of the data collection process to a minimum. The most effective positivist research will be able to be replicated by others, as with experiments in the natural sciences, or at least compared closely with other similar studies. For these reasons positivist researchers prefer structured methods of data collection which can be carried out on a large scale (macro studies). The data favoured are quantitative, usually presented as statistical tables, enabling others to see how the data have been interpreted and allowing for more accurate comparisons. The aim is to be able to generalise from the findings.

Certain criticisms have been levelled at the positivist paradigm and the use of statistics in social research:

1. Statistics will indicate trends but will not explain why people have done or said certain things. Since they do not yield detailed accounts of people's reasons the meanings obtained from statistical data remain superficial. Statistics of truancy, absence or examination success may show interesting trends but it is the stories behind them that will explain these trends. In this way statistics may be seen as impersonal. Positivist methods may ignore the richness of detailed individual accounts.
2. Statistical correlations should not be confused with causality. We could discern a correlation between the levels of umbrella carrying and car wiper blades operating but they are not causally linked; rather, both are consequent upon rainfall levels. A facetious example perhaps, but similarly there may be statistical relations between social deprivation and a lack of educational success. However, we need to go further than statistical analysis to see if the link is real and to seek explanations.

3. Statistical tables and analysis may appear to be objective but the choices researchers make in their compilations must not be overlooked. A researcher decides what to look for, asks certain questions yet ignores others, and collects, collates, interprets and categorises the data. There appears little likelihood of the whole process being unaffected by human contamination (see Cohen et al., 2007). Consider the construction of performance tables and how the data can be compiled in different ways to give very different impressions. Usher and Edwards (2000) provide strong theoretical grounds for challenging the objectivity and scientific claims of positivist approaches to education research.

Interpretivist paradigm

This paradigm embraces many social perspectives, notably phenomenology, symbolic interactionism, and ethnomethodology (see Flick, 2002; Denscombe, 2003). It does not see society as having a fixed structure, hidden or otherwise, because the social world is created by the interactions of individuals. Norms and values exist but as shifting organic elements of social life. They are used and changed by people as they interpret and respond to events. There are external pressures upon individuals but they do not act as some sort of external system controlling people. Weber (see Cuff and Payne et al., 1984; Hammersley, 2002) maintained that actions must be seen as meaningful at the level of interaction. By this he meant that action is taken to be deliberate and meaningful to those involved and the interpretivist paradigm seeks to understand the meanings behind these actions.

The interpretivist tries to show how choices are made by participants or 'actors' in social situations within the process of interaction. For the interpretivist there is no one objective reality that exists outside of the actor's explanations, just different versions of events. Pupils, the classroom teacher, other teachers at the school, parents, all have a view of what goes on and will act according to how they interpret events. The researcher in this paradigm seeks to 'understand' these actions.

Interpretivists prefer more 'naturalistic' forms of data collection, making use of individual accounts and biographies and often including detailed descriptions to give a 'feeling' for the environment. Methods favoured in interpretivist studies are informal interviews and observations which allow the situation to be as 'normal' as possible. These methods are often reliant upon the ability of the researcher to be reflexive in the research process. Interpretivist studies tend to be small scale (micro), aiming for detail and understanding rather than statistical representativeness. Whilst it is not possible to generalise from such studies researchers in this paradigm do attempt to be as rigorous as possible.

Woods suggests that qualitative research focuses on natural settings and is 'concerned with life as it is lived, things as they happen, situations as they are constructed in the day-to-day, moment-to-moment course of events'

(2006: 2). The researcher seeks to understand and portray the participants' perceptions and understandings of a particular situation or event. Interaction is ongoing and there is a continuing chain of events which gives insight into how people live with the research emphasising this process. Woods (2006) also cites the important part played by inductive analysis and grounded theory in qualitative research. The term 'grounded theory' comes from the work of Glaser and Strauss (1967) who suggested that in qualitative studies the researchers do not begin by hoping to prove or disprove a set hypothesis. They may have ideas on how 'things will go' but the theory must come from the data collected after the research has begun. It is 'grounded' in the data and the experiences of the researcher rather than being imposed upon the research before its commencement.

In summary, Yates (2004: 138) says that qualitative research attempts to do one or more of the following:

- Achieve an in-depth understanding and detailed description of a particular aspect of an individual, a case history or a group's experience(s).
- Explore how individuals or group members give meaning to and express their understanding of themselves, their experiences and/or their worlds.
- Find out and describe in detail social events and explore why they are happening, rather than how often.
- Explore the complexity, ambiguity and specific detailed processes taking place in a social context.

We can see that the qualitative methods used in social science research are readily applicable in the context of many education researchers.

Ethnography

This is a research strategy sometimes adopted by interpretivists which developed from anthropological studies of small-scale societies (Silverman, 2005). Ethnography is characterised by 'thick' descriptive accounts of the activities of particular groups studied. Accounts focus on the micro, spending much time looking at small groups and particular institutions.

For Walford (2001), ethnography takes into account the wider cultural context in which individuals or groups exist and live, as part of seeking to understand their behaviour and values. Fieldwork takes numerous forms and researchers will gather data from many sources, with a particular reliance on 'naturalistic' interpretive methods such as participant observation and informal interviews. This is in order to develop a multidimensional appreciation of these cultures and individuals. The researcher must have a long-term engagement with the situation to observe developments first hand and to experience the culture. Paradoxically the researcher should also attempt to view cultures dispassionately and to step outside their situation at times, what has been termed as viewing situations as 'anthropologically strange' (see Hammersley and Atkinson, 2007). Thus Walford (2001) sees ethnographic researchers developing their theoretical accounts over time as they conduct their ethnography. The aim is to construct an account that gives a deep and rich appreciation of the people who have been studied. Central to the description and analysis in ethnography are the views and perceptions of the actors. This research strategy, then, studies groups and individuals in their natural settings, considers the perspectives of those involved and the culture they are living in, uses a wide range of methods to develop a deep understanding and produces accounts which both the actors and researchers can recognise.

It therefore has much to offer those who are able to become immersed in the research field. For example, teachers, lecturers or instructors as researchers are part of the classroom situation, they are aware of the complex social interaction that takes place. Much of what they are interested in studying, concerning learning and development, needs to be understood in the context of daily institutional life and this in turn must be part of any explanation. They are also in a position to gather data over a long period and can often look to a variety of sources such as brief observations, snatched chats, as well as the more structured observations and interviews. They can keep records, mark work and speak with learners as individuals and groups. They will have colleagues who may also gather data. There is also the opportunity to photograph, video and record. Most significantly, those involved in the learning proces will be aware that the quality of data gathered is a reflection of the relationship and understanding between the students and the researcher. This understanding is a key part of the ethnographic research approach.

 Student Activity

Criticising qualitative research

Inevitably there have been criticisms of qualitative research and these have found particular expression within a policy context intent on 'driving up standards'. Policy makers felt that interpretivist approaches failed to provide clear-cut solutions, presenting instead an overly complex analysis of educational issues (see Lather, 2004, for further discussion).

Consider why such criticisms may be relatively easy to make.

Approaches to the research process and the type of data considered acceptable will very much depend upon how those carrying out the research see the world. Much falls within and between the two paradigms of positivism and interpretivism but sometimes this dichotomy can prove rather too simplistic, ignoring a multitude of variations. Several proponents of action research suggest that this two-paradigm view of research emanates from a traditional academic approach and they are critical of its application to professionally-based research. McNiff (2002), for instance, suggests critical theoretical and living theory approaches as being more appropriate. Clough and Nutbrown suggest that research studies often move between these paradigms selecting the most appropriate for different parts of a study. They propose that

> The issue is not so much a question of which paradigm to work within but how to dissolve that distinction in the interests of developing research design which serves the investigation of the questions posed through that research. (2007: 19)

Much practitioner research borrows from both major paradigms, using quantitative and/or qualitative methods as appropriate. Sometimes clear measures can be used and there will be a search for 'proof', whilst in other instances there is a need for interpretation and description that acknowledges the relativity of social life. It is certainly the case that whilst performance indicators are still used, for many researchers much of what is seen as the most important aspects of education cannot be measured in quantitative terms. Thus it is important for researchers to recognise the relevance of research paradigms in shaping how their projects are designed and conducted. This understanding could also help them to design imaginative research projects using a more eclectic approach.

Important research concepts

In undertaking a research project we need to consider some fundamental concepts that are of great significance in any piece of research. Thus we now turn to a discussion of the importance of reliability and validity. Triangulation is outlined as a significant strategy that can be applied in order to increase the validity of any findings.

Reliability

Reliability describes the extent to which a research instrument or method is repeatable. It is an assessment of the consistency of any method. Thus for Pole and Lampard (2002) the reliability of a measure is the extent to which respondents will consistently respond to it in the same way. Corbetta says that reliability marks:

> The degree to which a given procedure for transforming a concept into a variable produces the same results in tests repeated with the same empirical tools (stability) or equivalent ones (equivalence). (2003: 81)

In other words the more reliable the method of data collection the more likely it is to give similar results in subsequent administrations. An unreliable measure will yield different results every time it is administered (Anderson, 1998).

Positivist researchers who wish to carry out large-scale research are most concerned with reliability. The methods need to be capable of being applied to large numbers of respondents in order to generate the data required. To be able to make the desired statistical comparisons the collection of data needs to be consistent, namely, reliable. In contrast, the interpretivist researcher is likely to be more concerned with the suitability of the methods for eliciting qualitative, accurate and detailed accounts from each respondent. Thus the emphasis on reliability varies according to the paradigm of the researcher.

It should be noted that a high level in reliability in a data collection instrument does not necessarily mean that it is accurate. For instance, if a tutor asks students to evaluate a course by named questionnaire and they are aware that the tutor will shortly be marking their assignments, this is likely to concentrate their minds. Not surprisingly, the tutor will then have positive student feedback. Whilst this method can be said to be reliable, in that its questions are similarly understood by successive cohorts of students and thus it is always measuring the same thing, its accuracy in terms of the truthfulness of the student responses is certainly suspect.

Validity

Validity and its measurement play an important part in determining the appropriate methods to employ. Validity refers to the 'truthfulness', 'correctness', or accuracy of research data. If results are to be considered accurate then the research instrument must measure what we claim it is to measure. Thus 'an indicator is valid to the extent that it empirically represents the concept it purports to measure' (Punch, 2005: 100). For instance, tests of mathematical ability might actually be producing results which are indicative of the ability to read the questions rather than of mathematical prowess. If our methods are at fault then the findings will be invalid and the research worthless. In aiming to increase validity positivists emphasise the standardisation of data collection whilst using as large a sample as possible. Thus the piloting of any method for accuracy is very important.

Another approach to validity, more associated with an interpretivist approach, places an emphasis on the final account and how the researcher is able to defend the interpretations they make from the data (Punch, 2005). In other words, the researcher needs to show on what evidence they are basing their findings. This can be done in a number of ways, such as giving full explanations as to how data were gathered; member checks (Maykut and Morehouse, 1994), whereby research participants are asked if their accounts have been recorded accurately; and reducing researcher bias by giving a colleague samples of all the data collected to verify the analysis and conclusions drawn by the researcher (as suggested by Miles and Huberman, 1994). In action research the openness of the findings to scrutiny and discussion by fellow practitioners is seen as a significant part in ensuring the validity of what is often small-scale research carried out by researchers who are themselves part of the research project (McNiff, 2002).

Triangulation

Triangulation is a navigational term which means to fix one's position from two known bearings. This process is carried out by researchers to increase the validity of their research and it means checking one's findings by using several points of reference. In effect, the researcher is approaching the object of the research from as many different angles and perspectives as possible in order to gain a greater understanding. Researchers can triangulate by using a number of different fieldworkers in the collection and analysis of data – seeking, the contribution of varied groups of respondents such as pupils, teachers and parents, using a range of research methods, considering qualitative and quantitative data, and so on. Miles and Huberman pointed to triangulation as a way of life. If findings were consciously checked and double-checked using different sources of evidence then the verification would be built in

> ... by seeing or hearing multiple instances of it from different sources, by using different methods and by squaring the finding with others it needs to be squared with. (1994: 267)

The positivist would hope to show a congruency of results from triangulation. The interpretivist would use the different sources of data to give greater depth to their analysis, corroborating or leading to a discussion of any variation in the findings (Silverman, 2005; Woods, 2006). Thus for Hammersley and Atkinson

> What is involved in triangulation is not the combination of different kinds of data per se, but rather an attempt to relate different sorts of data in such a way as to counteract various possible threats to the validity of our analysis. (2007: 232)

Certainly both paradigms would suggest the use of triangulation to increase the validity of their findings but would use it in slightly different ways. In order to produce a more thorough and rigorous piece of research several methods will often be used in conjunction with one another. The main methods, in fact, often complement each other. For instance, what has been seen during observations can be raised in interviews by the researcher. This will give an understanding of why something happened as well as a descriptive account. Triangulation is likely to appear as almost a natural process to researchers who are used to considering different viewpoints and obtaining data from several sources in order to more fully understand particular incidents or aspects of their focus.

Student Activity

Using different paradigms

1. Take one of the following research topics and consider firstly a positivist and then an interpretivist approach. Consider what each would be looking for in their research, the type of data they would collect, what would be considered appropriate methods and who the possible respondents would be.

   Research topics to consider: student achievement in higher education; pupil truancy; pupil transition from primary to secondary school; assessment of learning; the quality of nursery provision; teenage attitudes to vocational education.

   Please add any other topic that you think may be interesting.

2. Discuss your answers, noting any similarities and differences between the likely approaches of the two paradigms, and the effects of these upon the resulting research.

Conclusion

In this chapter we have considered how a researcher's position will influence the whole research process. We have identified the major paradigms but warned of the dangers of regarding these as in any way fixed and static. There are in fact many positionings that researchers can take and these are likely to change over their lifetime. We now look at the importance of ethics in designing and conducting your research project.

Recommend Reading

Benton, T. and Craib, I. (2001) *Philosophy of Social Science: The Philosophical Foundations of Social Thought.* Basingstoke: Palgrave. This is an excellent introduction to the philosophy of social sciences. It will give you a good introduction to epistemology, ontology, ethics and political philosophy and will then outline the major positions and debates in the social sciences. This is an ideal book to help you refine your own positioning.

Clough, P. and Nutbrown, C. (2007) *A Student's Guide to Methodology.* London: Sage. This text helps the reader to develop an understanding of the research process through a series of challenging activities that the authors have developed through their teaching. It encourages the novice researcher to seriously consider the nature of research from different perspectives.

Delanty, G. and Strydom, P. (eds) (2003) *Philosophies of Social Science: The Classic and Contemporary Readings*. Maidenhead: Open University Press. After an introduction to the philosophy of social science this collection uses key extracts from the original authors to consider questions of epistemology, methodology, and knowledge. As a new researcher it is always important to visit the initial sources and not just rely on secondhand accounts.

Ritzer, G. and Smart, B. (eds) (2001) *Handbook of Social Theory*. London: Sage. This edited book provides a comprehensive set of readings on social theory. These will be very useful in helping you to develop a deeper understanding of the different social perspectives. Some of the chapters are challenging for the novice but certainly well worth the effort.

3

An ethical approach to research

There are always ethical considerations that must be addressed before embarking upon a research project and taken into account whilst the project is ongoing.

Ethical awareness involves researchers demonstrating care and respect for all of those involved in and affected by their research. This chapter will explain why an ethical approach to research is essential. It will show the ethical considerations that researchers should make, paying partic- ular attention to conducting small-scale research projects. The process of gaining ethical consent will also be examined.

The growing awareness of the importance of ethical approaches to research

Ethics should be a central consideration for all education researchers. We need to be aware that research, if conducted without care and consideration, can have potentially harmful effects for those taking part. Researchers must consider the rights of the individual who may be giving data and they also need to ensure that all those taking part in the research and the information they provide are treated in a sensitive manner. All data need to remain confidential and the respondents need to be assured, as far as possible, that their anonynymity will be maintained unless agreed otherwise. Researchers must realise that the process of collecting data and knowledge can bestow on them a sense of power over others. It is important that they then behave in an appropriately respectful manner.

In recent years it has become mandatory for researchers in almost all universities and research organisations, when conducting their research and when applying for research funding from independent sources, to submit their proposals to formal ethical scrutiny and to obtain the approval of at least one, and sometimes several, official ethics committees. This was not the case even ten years ago and some of those who have been involved in research for many years still regard this requirement as both an imposition and a restriction on their ability to conduct research. Ethics procedures may be seen by such researchers as a curtailment of their freedom to carry out research that they view as appropriate whenever and however they want. The gaining of ethical approval is, from this perspective, seen as a hurdle to be overcome.

Whilst the relationship between those serving on ethics committees and researchers putting forward proposals is sometimes portrayed as confrontational, this should not detract from the importance of adopting an ethical approach to research per se. Ethics committees are essentially there to help maintain the confidence of both the academic and non-academic community in the standards by which research is conducted. We argue below that ethical considerations are a vital part of any research. To deliberately ignore them or pretend they don't exist promotes a shallow or even a deficient approach to research.

What are ethics?

The term comes from the Greek *ethos*, meaning 'character'. There are various definitions that can be used.

> Ethics is the systematic study of value concepts – 'good', 'bad', 'right', 'wrong' – and the general principles that justify applying these concepts (Sieber, 1992: 3).
> Ethics 'is concerned with perspectives on right and proper conduct' (Israel and Hay, 2006: 12).

Israel and Hay suggest that it is the goodwill of individuals and social groups that allows us to conduct research. We do not have an automatic right to expect this and it is a privilege that can be easily withdrawn if researchers behave in ways that are harmful, unjust, or insensitive to the needs of those communities in which they are working. It is only from a position of trust that researchers are able to continue their work.

 Student Activity

Being concerned with ethics is an important moral position and is about the integrity of both the research and the researcher.

> We behave in ways that are right and virtuous: for the sake of those who put trust in us and our work. (Israel and Hay, 2006: 10)

Consider whether the integrity needed by you as a researcher may inhibit what you wish to achieve. How will you avoid this happening?

Ethical principles

There can be various ethical positions that can be taken. Consequentialist approaches, for instance, will weigh the balance between the good and bad consequences of actions. They will consider an action to be morally right if the resulting benefits outweigh the risks of either not acting or doing something different. The adoption of this utilitarian approach, though seeming straightforward at first sight, can however, sometimes lead to problems. The difficulty here is in deciding 'good for whom?'. Thus what is good for society may not be best for individuals, or may even be to their disadvantage. For instance, allowing child labour may enable goods to be produced more cheaply for the benefit of the society and the good of the economy but it may significantly blight the lives of child workers.

Deontological approaches do not look at effect in particular, but see some actions as good in themselves, e.g. maintaining confidentiality. This approach emphasises 'doing what is right', i.e. treating others as you would wish to be treated. This position is taken on the basis of the morality of the action regardless of the consequences. However, whilst this approach appears highly correct it can also cause problems in particular cases, for instance, when you have promised confidentiality but then discover something that you really feel needs to be disclosed. Thus if you are told during an interview that an adult is abusing young children wouldn't it surely be right to go to the authorities even though you had promised confidentiality?

Thus behaving ethically is not always as straightforward as it seems initially. Consider the position of doctors who have to make life and death decisions on such things as whether to turn off life support systems that keep unconcious patients alive. They need to consider all the medical aspects of each individual case. It may not be possible to come to a universally applicable decision on these issues as they involve the balancing of complex facts to make a judgement, but the important thing is to be open about the issues – to debate them, to show the rationale behind each decision and to always behave in a morally justifiable way. Therefore behaving ethically is a code for living and so the same principles apply when conducting reseach.

In the USA the National Commission for the Protection of Human Subjects in Biomedical and Behavioural Science identified ethical principles in the Belmont Report in 1979 that continue to strongly influence ethics committees in the UK. Three principles were identified to guide research involving human subjects.

Beneficence

This principle involves maximising benefits whilst minimising harm. This can, as mentioned above, lead to difficult cost benefit debates.

(Continued)

(Continued)

Justice
Procedures should be fair and reasonable. Equals should be treated equally (i.e. no one should suffer whilst others gain). This principle is significant for an example given later in this chapter on opportunities given to some pupils but denied to others as part of an experiment.

Respect for persons
The autonomy of individuals should be recognised and individual rights respected.

The Council for International Organisations of Medical Sciences (CIOMS)(1982, revised in 1993 and 2002) published its own code of ethics that is very similar to the Belmont Report. When considering research conducted in poorer countries, it added to 'respect for persons' that investigators should not make unjust conditions worse or take advantage of vulnerable populations. By this they were thinking of instances such as chemical companies testing new drugs on poorly paid volunteers in the Third World, thereby taking advantage of their poverty and the lack of legal safeguards in their countries to protect them against such exploitation by multinational companies.

The CIOMS also stressed the need for formal scrutiny of proposed research, thus encouraging the rapid development of ethics committees from this time onwards.

Applications of ethical principles

The application of such principles usually involves consideration of certain key aspects of any research proposal, which all researchers including students must submit to.

1. Informed consent

It is usual to seek the consent of those involved in the research. This sounds easier to obtain than it sometimes actually is. It necessitates a consideration of who actually needs to give consent, whether this needs to be recorded, and the understandings of the respondents concerning the nature of the research and their ability to withdraw from it if they so decide even after initially giving consent. How explicitly and formally each of these points need to be addressed varies from research project to research project. For instance, students taking part in research at a university are all adults and would expect to be asked for their consent individually. It would depend upon the nature of the research as to whether permission from the university itself needs to be sought, though it may be considered reasonable to consult university staff at particular levels (thus asking Deans, or department heads, or module tutors as appropriate). For research involving school pupils the position is much more complicated. In the first instance the school, usually in the person of the head teacher, must give consent for any research taking place within that school. It may be appropriate to seek parental permission depending upon the nature of the research, and/or the consent of the individual pupils may also be sought. Teachers should also be consulted if the research takes place in their classrooms, especially if it involves their teaching.

This may all seem very complicated but the factors that determine the levels of consent required by ethics committees before research can be conducted in schools are, generally,

- the nature of the topic being investigated;
- the age of the pupils/respondents and their ability to make an informed judgement of their consent;

Certainly it would be worth while to discuss the research and any findings with the pupils/students involved at some point, if only to reflect upon any changes or developments that have resulted from the focus of the investigation, such as how their work has improved, how the organisation of the classroom has changed, and so on.

Researchers also need to keep in mind that consent is given by the respondent to use the data gathered from them for a particular research project. This does not mean that the researcher can automatically use the data in other research projects without asking further permission.

2. Confidentiality and privacy

Usually confidentiality relating to any information given and the privacy of the respondents is guaranteed by the researcher through a promise of anonymity. The researcher needs to consider how identifiable individuals are or are likely to be in the findings. It must not be assumed that just because names are not mentioned then someone cannot be identified as taking part in the research. For instance, if a case study is being done of one institution, such as a school, then anyone knowing research has been done here and reading the report can guess who the individual contributions are from or can at least narrow the possibilities down. So if the report states something like 'the head teacher stated that ... ', 'a female deputy head thought that ... ', 'a male teacher in the 50 to 60 age group expressed annoyance that ...', then the respondents may feel that their anonymity has not been maintained and so the promise of confidentiality has been compromised.

What would happen in instances of disclosure during interviews or the likelihood of any disclosure taking place needs to be considered beforehand by the researcher. For instance, unintentionally discovering through interviews information concerning the drug use, sexual activity or other deviant behaviour of pupils has always presented researchers with the dilemma of protecting confidential sources or reporting such activity to parents and the 'authorities'. What a researcher may do is, whilst promising confidentiality, state that that they also have a duty of care to disclose any illegal or criminal activity raised during the interview to a suitable authority or third person. This is likely to avoid interviewees deliberately mentioning such things for bravado purposes or to deliberately embarass the interviewer.

The researcher will also need to consider and state what will happen to the data after these have been collected, i.e. how it will be stored, if it will be destroyed after a period of time, if it may be used in other studies, how the research findings might be reported in the public domain.

3. Honesty and openness
Whilst not wishing their presence to influence the behaviour of the respondents unduly, researchers need to consider how open they can make the research process. Certainly deception can prove to be counter-productive in the long term as well as being morally objectionable. Much of the classroom research carried out by teachers, for example, actually benefits from being open and involving others.

4. Access to findings
It is an important principle that any final report or submission of findings is presented to the respondents or is at least made accessible to them. Certainly seeking confirmation from respondents is a part of the validation process for many of the methods discussed in this book. As well as strengthening the validity of the findings, feedback from those involved is often an important part of the research process.

5. Avoiding harm (doing good)
This involves an assesment of any harm (or benefits) that the research may cause. It is important that you as a researcher are considered able to conduct the research in a way that does not cause undue stress, harm or inconvenience to the respondents. The safety of researchers and any members of the research team must also be an important consideration. This may certainly involve scrutiny of different parts of the design of the research proposal by an ethics committee. There follows an example of a research project that was considered unacceptable by an ethics committee for a number of reasons.

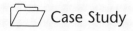 Case Study

An undergraduate student was aware of the publicity surrounding the under achievement of African Caribbean pupils. She proposed to carry out research in a multi-ethnic primary school to find out why this was the case. She hoped to observe pupils in lessons and to interview African Caribbean pupils about their experiences at school and also about their future expectations.

Ethical approval for this research could not be given on a number of grounds. The student seemed unaware of the sensitivity and understanding needed to research such issues. She did not realise the concern and distress that could be caused to the pupils, the teachers and the parents by a stranger probing such significant aspects of their lives. It did not occur to her to consider how they would react.

The student also did not show a reasonable understanding of the issue she was investigating and just assumed that the newspaper headlines were correct. If she had been familiar with current research she would have realised that the under achievement of pupils of African Caribbean descent is not as clear-cut as may be perceived, especially in primary schools, through reading sensationalist stories. Thus, although this is a significant issue to research that should be investigated, it was not considered appropriate for such an inexperienced researcher.

A different approach by this student may have been much more acceptable. For instance she could have looked at how the school attempted to pursue a multicultural teaching policy. This would have allowed her to examine the curriculum, wall displays and pupil work, and to interview teachers. She could have had discussions with groups of pupils about what they did at school. This – while not the focus she originally wished to research – would have been a more positive approach for her to take. It would also have been more acceptable to the school that was proud of its inclusive ethos and would have been more appropriate for the skills of an undergraduate researcher.

 ## Student Activity

Consider the two research proposals below that were submitted to an ethics committee.

- What do you think are the key issues in each proposal that the researchers and ethics committee should consider and why?
- If you were on the ethics committee discussing each proposal with the researcher is there anything that you would like more details or information on to do with the project?
- If you were on the ethics committee what would you be looking for to ensure that such research was carried out ethically?

It is important to note that in each of these examples the researcher was conducting research at PhD level, they had previous experience of conducting research and they were to be supervised by experienced researchers in their particular field.

(Continued)

(Continued)

Case Study 1

A case study into children's perspectives on the Early Years curriculum

This will be an exploration into how young children depict their experience of the nursery school. Ten children in a class at one day care centre will be the respondents (two–three years old).

The researcher will spend several days per week before the commencement of the research becoming acquainted with the children and the setting and allowing them to get to know her. The actual research will take place over five months for three days per week.

The research is characterised as an ethnographic case study. The children will be involved in all stages of the research and have a say in what data they want and don't want to be collected.

Methods of data collection

Video of activities of the children (half an hour three days per week).
Field notes (mornings, three days per week).
Personal diary compiled by the researcher filled in after every day.
Daily diary constructed by the children with the help of the adults working in the setting (this is an activity that the children currently do).
Photographs taken by the children and the researcher (older children can act as helpers).
Voice recordings made by the children.
Interviews of parents, teachers and children.
All photos and recordings will be played back to the children every week for them to approve/check/pass comment.

Case 2

An exploration of the transformative potential of university for disabled students

A participatory/emancipatory approach will be taken to the research.
It will examine whether disabled students have their sense of identity altered by university and if so how.
The main phase of the research will involve approximately ten disabled students in interviews.
Respondents will be recruited through consultation with the Student Enabling Centre at the university.
Data will be collected via individual interview and focus group sessions over a period of 12 months.
Respondents will be invited to review and comment on their contribution to the project.
Data will be destroyed after the project is complete.

Formal ethical guidance

Any prospective researcher would do well to consult the *Ethical Guidelines for Educational Research* produced by the British Educational Research Association (BERA, 2004). In suggesting 'that all educational research should be conducted within an ethic of respect for:

- the person;
- knowledge;
- democratic values; and
- the quality of educational research' (BERA, 2004: 3)

BERA sets out the guidelines concerning researchers' responsibilities to participants in research, to sponsors of research, and to the wider community of educational researchers.

An interesting example of an ethical issue affecting a research proposal is highlighted in the following scenario.

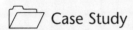 Case Study

> A teacher had access to a very sophisticated IT package that appeared to have great potential for developing the literacy, IT capabilities and communication skills of young children. This was also a package that the teacher felt sure the pupils would find enjoyable and would therefore also have long-term motivational benefits.
>
> There were two parallel classes in Year 1 at the school, and the teacher was proposing to run the package with one of the classes as part of their literacy programme. This would be the experimental group and their academic development would be closely monitored. A second class was to be taught literacy using the traditional format and was not to have the use of the IT package. The performance of this group was also to be monitored and the pupils would act as a comparison or control group.

The concerns that this example raises are focused around school resources being used for the benefit of one class of pupils and not the other. The control group would be likely, and quite reasonably, to feel discriminated against. How would parents of children in the control class in particular react to pupils being treated so differently? They may feel that their children were being deprived of educational opportunities. It would seem inexcusable for the parents not to be told of such research and if not officially informed they are likely to be even more annoyed once they found out unofficially.

This example shows the ethical questions that can confound the use of experimental and control groups in education research. In this example the research would have useful aims in wishing to examine the effects of an IT package. However, it could have been designed in such a way that pupils were not split into distinct experimental and control groups concerning the use of such a desirable facility. Pupil use of the package could be evaluated on a more individual basis and each child's progress monitored.

The work of ethics committees

We have said previously that all research proposals need to go before ethics committees. As you may realise from the above examples these committees operate with a duty of care for the respondents/participants in the research and also the researchers. The ethical approval process should therefore be seen as supportive of quality research rather than a hindrance that has to be overcome or got round. Going through some form of ethical scrutiny means that other, experienced researchers will examine a proposal and as a result of their comments and recommendations the final research design will invariably become stronger. Practice and procedure vary, but usually where the research is considered to be relatively straightforward with few ethical risks or issues the procedure for gaining ethical approval is administered with a light touch. Where there are more significant ethical considerations to be addressed then the ethical scrutiny will tend to be greater. It is usual that universities do not allow undergraduates to conduct research that involves more than minimal risk due to the novice status of such researchers.

Student Activity

Identifying ethical procedures

If you are studying at an HE institution, obtain a copy of its ethical guidelines for research. Discuss the policy of the institution and any procedures in place to monitor the ethics of research projects.

Conclusion

This chapter has considered the importance of adopting an ethical stance in conducting research. It has outlined a number of ethical dilemmas that you may come upon and has explained the procedures for applying fundamental ethical principles.

Those of us working and researching in fields such as education, social work and medicine are continually presented with ethical dilemmas. It is important that all researchers take an ethical stance in their research and only act in a way that they can morally justify, even though this may not always be easy (see Oliver, 2003, for a discussion of this).

Recommended Reading

BERA (2004) *Revised Ethical Guidelines for Educational Research*. Nottingham: British Educational Research Association. BERA produces a range of very helpful guides for education researchers which you can access at its website http://www.bera.ac.uk/

Campbell, A. and Groundwater-Smith, S. (2007) *An Ethical Approach to Practitioner Research: Dealing with Issues and Dilemmas in Action Research*. Abingdon: Routledge. This is a fascinating international collection of education research studies discussed from the point of view of their ethical implications.

Oliver, P. (2003) *The Student's Guide to Research Ethics*. Maidenhead: Open University Press. This text introduces the reader to ethical issues that occur in research. It considers every stage of the research process from design to writing the final report. This is a very accessible volume that covers an area that must be addressed by all researchers.

Pring, R. (2004) *Philosophy of Educational Research* (second edition). London: Continuum. This is very interesting book on the philosophy of educational research. The chapter on research ethics is particularly useful.

Getting started: beginning a research project

This chapter outlines the initial planning that is required if a research project is to be carried out successfully. Before embarking on the research process the researcher needs to have carefully thought through the purpose and precise focus of the research. These are key factors that will shape the whole project. They will determine the scale, detail and writing up of the final results. In this chapter we will also discuss the setting of a research focus, asking research questions and project planning.

Designing a research project

As a researcher you will need to turn your initial ideas into a research outline/strategy. This is usually termed a 'research proposal' when applying for grants, funding, or admission to a research degree programme. There is a need to construct a structured plan that identifies what is going to be investigated, how the research will be carried out, and what will be the expected outcomes in terms of data and analysis. This all needs to be put in a time frame, so a detailed timeline needs to be written that sets targets to work towards.

Whilst it is important to have a clear plan by which to operate, this must not be allowed to become too rigid. Any researcher must be prepared to adapt and change according to altering circumstances. Many things may happen concerning the focus of the research or your circumstances as researcher that can cause substantial alterations to the original plans. Sometimes the final research project will be very different from that which you initially intended. However, it is useful to start with as clear a plan as possible. This will at least give you a feeling of security at the start of what can be perceived as a rather risky and threatening process. (See Punch, 1998, for a further discussion of how to develop research proposals.)

Research is about asking questions (Clough and Nutbrown, 2007) and then gathering data to help answer these questions. However, this can develop into an ever-expanding process if not managed effectively. It is possible to ask what seems like a never-ending stream of questions that become progressively wider in scope and leave you feeling very unclear about where the research should be going. What is needed initially is to develop a clear focus of investigation. Ideally, it should be possible to explain the focus in a paragraph which states what is to be researched and why. By having a focus, or a main aim/purpose, it should then be possible to ask what it is you specifically want to find out concerning this focus – namely, what the particular issues are. This will highlight the important questions to which you need to find the answers: in other words, the key research questions.

At the same time, give some thought as to a title for the research project. This will become easier to write as the focus becomes clearer. A good title should signify clearly and concisely the topic of the research and the target group that make up the respondents. It should indicate the parameters of the research, for example, clarifying whether it is a case study involving one example or whether it involves large samples.

Research questions

You should work up the key research questions at the same time as the focus and title. All three – focus, title and research questions – are part of the initial developments of the research proposal.

So what are research questions?

These are questions that require researchers to 'define the limits of their study, clarify their research study, identify empirical issues and work on empirical questions' (Clough and Nutbrown, 2002: 33).

They identify precisely which aspects of the area of interest should be researched, and they indicate the sources from which information can/should be obtained and also the appropriate ways of collecting this information (Lewis and Munn, 1997).

We will now consider how research questions can be developed from a particular focus.

Student transition into Higher Education: an example of designing research

Entering Higher Education (HE) and becoming a student represents a milestone in anyone's life. For many young people it is the first time they will have lived away from home for any significant period. This is bound to be quite an emotional time for both new students and also those they leave behind. Entering Higher Education for many, whether living at home or 'away', signifies a big step along the road of making one's own way in the world. It is moving from school-based learning into the more independent and adult world of higher learning. Whilst considered an exciting time of personal development it can also be a period of uncertainty, self-doubt and even fear.

Being aware of this and having already lived through their first two years of a three-year degree programme, a group of final year students studying Education Studies as part of a joint awards programme at one particular university, decided to do research into the process of student transition into Higher Education. To make this small-scale piece of research manageable they decided to study students from their own faculty at the university. Apart from just investigating the experiences of students similar to themselves they wanted to highlight the problems encountered during this period as well as celebrating the positives. It was hoped that by understanding the process clear strategies could be proposed that would make the transition smoother.

During an initial thought-sharing session they realised that there were many areas that could be worth investigating that were to do with student transition, such as worries over accommodation, concerns about courses and aspects of study at university, fears about getting into debt and changing relationships with old friends and family. These needed to be arranged into groups or clusters in a logical fashion that made sense to the researchers. They could also make decisions about the areas they did want to investigate and if there were any they didn't. By the end of the initial session the group had identified a series of research questions:

1. What are the experiences of students in this faculty during their first six months of study?
2. How have they coped and how settled do they feel now?
3. What could be done in future to help new students settle in more?

These can be seen as a first attempt at designing a set of research questions. They may change as the research progresses – they may be refined, added to, and so on. By formulating research questions the research team is beginning to put some structure around their focus and is now in a position to develop a plan to carry out the research. In this particular case three main questions have been asked with sub-questions within them. It is clear from this that three distinct things need to be found out: Q1. *What are the experiences of students in their first few months of study?* This involves sub-questions focusing on how the reality compares with their fears and expectations. When there is a clearer idea of what is happening it becomes possible to find out *how these students manage to cope with the transition into HE* (Q2). This can only be done when the true extent of the issues are known. On the basis of data gathered from the first two questions *what can be done for future students* can then be explored (Q3).

The research questions have now provided a clear trail to follow – it is possible to identify what data need to be gathered and who they should be collected from. That leads to the next step, which is designing the appropriate methods by which to gather these data. There is thus a progression from developing research

Table 4.1   Data Collection Plan for Student Experiences Research

Research Questions	Sources	Methods
1. What are the experiences of students on entering HE?	University retention data Students Student welfare officer	Descriptive statistical analysis Questionnaires/interviews Interviews
2. How have they coped and how settled do they feel now?	Students Student welfare officer	Interviews/questionnaire Interviews
3. What can be done in future to help students settle in more?	Students Staff Student welfare officer	Questionnaires/interviews Interviews Interviews

questions, to identifying the data needed to answer these questions, to designing appropriate methods that can be used to gather the data.

Though respondents and data collection instruments have been identified important decisions still have to be made. Whilst it is possible to say that responses will be gathered from students, lecturers and student welfare officers, it still needs to be decided which of these will be included in the research sample. It may also be difficult to obtain data from students on what for some may be a sensitive issue. Here the data collection methods decided upon and the skills of the researchers become important to the outcomes of the research. It is also easy to identify interviews and questionnaires as the main methods to be used but actually designing them can prove more difficult. As this is a first draft of the plan it is likely that there will be a number of changes as the researchers learn more about student experiences and are able to reflect upon their research as it develops. They may decide that some of the methods listed need to be carefully adapted to be more sensitive to the respondents. Other sources of useful data may also come to mind, e.g. the experiences and opinions of parents, second and third year students, those who have graduated, and university counsellors may be sought.

Once the research questions have been developed it becomes possible to draw up a clear plan that the researchers can work with and which can be refined and developed over time. They need to consider practical research issues where the outcomes to these will be linked to the intended size of the project, such as the time and skills needed to design the various research methods, the collection and analysis of the data, and the presentation of findings. These form the content of the following chapters of this book. Alongside this practical planning of the research process within their university, the researchers will be aware of the need to draw on wider experiences. Other universities are likely to have tackled the problem of transition of students to university and it would help to know if they carried out their own research and if so how they did it and what they found. It would also help to know what national and even international research has been done, what conclusions had been drawn, what strategies had been tried, and how successful these had been. Thus there is a need to carry out a literature search to inform the research project being developed. With any piece of research, a literature review forms a valuable section. Literature informs the compiling of research questions and research questions help, in turn, to identify areas of literature that need to be reviewed. The process of literature searches will be dealt with in Chapter 5.

Let us consider another example of designing a research project. This example was a group of teachers wishing to explore a problem that existed within their school. This is very much an area of professional concern and the teachers will need to be aware of the ethical issues to be addressed when researching such a topic. (Ethical approaches to research were examined in detail in Chapter 3.)

Pupil truancy: Designing a research project

In one secondary school staff had become aware of an increasing truancy problem. This had always been an issue, but the problem had been specifically raised in a staff meeting by one of the pastoral heads. Open discussion among staff then indicated certain worrying trends that some teachers had noticed, such as an apparent increase in the number of pupils on the corridors during lesson time and instances of when some pupils had not been in lessons when teachers had seen them earlier in the day. It was also reported that local shop-keepers had rung the school concerning pupils in school uniform 'hanging around' the local shopping centre during school hours. Thus truancy of pupils during school hours had become identified as an issue needing investigation to be followed by effective action.

At this point an action group has been formed and in its initial meeting the following series of research questions have arisen via a discussion and brain-storming session. We can place these into major and sub-questions:

1. What is the current extent of pupil truancy?

   - How many pupils are truanting?
   - Which pupils are truanting (boys, girls, age, ability)?
   - When are these pupils truanting?
   - How frequently does this happen?
   - For how long do they truant?

2. Why are pupils truanting?

   - Is there an issue with particular lessons?
   - What part does peer pressure play on truanting?
   - Is truancy related to academic progress? If so, is it a result or cause of poor performance by truants?
   - To what extent is truancy related to wider social issues outside school?
   - Do their parents or other adults know of their truancy?

3. What do truants do?

   - Where do they go?
   - Are they usually alone, or with friends who are also truanting?

- Are they involved in delinquent or criminal activity whilst truanting?
- Are they working for money whilst truanting?

4. What can be done to tackle the problem of truancy?
   - What are the suggestions of staff, pupils, parents?
   - What have other schools tried and how successful have they been?
   - What suggestions have come from national and international research?

These form the initial set of research questions. In this particular case, four main questions have been asked with sub-questions within them. It is clear from this that four distinct things need to be found out: Q1. *What is the extent of the problem?* (This involves the sub-questions of who, when, how often?) When there is a clearer idea of what is happening and who is taking part it then becomes possible to find out *why these pupils are truanting* (Q2). Note that this can only be done when the true extent of the problem is known, as many truants will be missed in the research if data are only gathered from particularly high profile pupils, who are already known as truants to the staff. Linked to the question of why pupils truant is the issue of *what they do whilst truanting* (Q3). On the basis of data gathered from the first three questions *what can be done to tackle the problem* can then be explored (Q4).

These research questions have provided a clear trail to follow. They help to identify what data need to be gathered, who to collect those from and how this can be done. At this stage appropriate methods can now be designed by which the data can be gathered.

As with the previous example, important decisions will still have to be made as to which pupils and teachers will be included in the research sample. It may also be difficult to obtain data from pupils on such an issue and the researchers will need to ensure that the data collection methods used are carefully adapted to be more sensitive to the respondents. Certainly the consent of those taking part in the research will have to be carefully sought. Here the

Table 4.2   Data Collection Plan for Truancy Research

Research Questions	Sources	Methods
1. What is the extent of truancy in school X?	Staff, pupils	Attendance checks Cameras, corridor sweeps, pupil interviews, staff interviews

(a) How many pupils are truanting?
   (b) Which pupils are truanting – boys, girls, age, ability?
   (c) When are these pupils truanting?
   (d) How frequently?
   (e) For how long do they truant?		

2. Why are pupils truanting?	Staff, pupils	Interviews/questionnaire
3. What do truants do?	Pupils	Interviews
4. What can be done to tackle the problem of truancy?	Staff, pupils, parents	Interviews/questionnaire

data collection methods decided upon and the skills of the researcher will become important to the outcomes of the research. As this is a first draft of the plan it is likely that there will be a number of changes as the teacher researchers learn more about truancy and are able to reflect upon their research as it develops. Other sources of useful data may also come to mind, e.g. the experiences and opinions of parents, social services, youth workers and the police may be sought, together with those of the local shopkeepers who initially reported the issue.

Alongside this practical planning of the research process within the school, the action group will be aware that other schools are likely to have tackled the problem of truancy and it would help to know if they carried out their own research and if so how they did it and what was the result. It would also help to know what national and even international research has been done, what conclusions had been drawn, what strategies had been tried and how successful these had been. Thus there is a need to carry out a literature search to inform the research project being developed.

There is the potential here for a continuing spiral of practitioner research to be created from an initial investigation such as this. Various strategies for reducing truancy are likely to be suggested in answer to research question 4. The next stage would be to implement these, with the teachers themselves evaluating their effectiveness through further research.

Having considered the design of research projects we can identify some general guidelines on the forming of research questions. Research questions result from a process of thinking through and possibly discussing the issue to be investigated.

Useful prompts which help in the framing of research questions include:

- Why research this area?
- What precisely is it that we want to find out about?
- Is there a desire to change anything? If so, what and why?
- What/who are the likely sources of information and data?
- What are the views of other researchers/colleagues/peers on this research focus and what are their initial reactions to the study?
- What are the issues identified in the literature?
- What are the key findings of any research already done?

Research timeline

With the title written, the research focus clear, research questions in place and a literature search underway, it is now possible to construct a timeline for the project. This will identify an order in which things can be done and give a realistic length of time in which to do them. A clear plan helps to ensure that nothing important has been missed out. It gives you, as the researcher, a programme to work through and a realistic completion date. This should enable you to feel more in control of the process and able to manage the stress of deadlines. It should also allow you to fit the research into existing work commitments. A plan, providing it is continually reviewed, actually enables you to be more flexible and to adapt to unforeseen circumstances more effectively

An example of a research timeline

Julie, a final year Education Studies undergraduate, wanted to study the learning experiences of first year Education Studies students for her dissertation. She had been very interested in the learning process since she came to university from her school sixth form. She had realised the great differences in how they were now taught and expected to learn because of her own experiences when she had studied for her A levels as compared to starting her degree. Though she had studied learning theories as part of her degree programme, the final year dissertation gave her the opportunity to investigate student learning experiences in more depth. Julie had discussed the project with her supervisor, developed her research questions, and conducted her literature review in the first semester. She was going to conduct the research and write up the findings in the second semester before the mid May hand-in deadline.

One advantage she felt she had was that being a third year student she knew many of the lecturers and students and was familiar with the course and university facilities. She was hoping to collect data through a questionnaire given to first year Education Studies students about their experiences across their programme, then conduct a focus group of about six to ten students, and lastly interview three lecturers who were teaching first year Education Studies students. Her worry was how to do all of this within one semester. Julie had designed a timeline in her first semester after considering the following questions posed by her tutor:

- How are you going to organise your time to carry out the research?
- When will you have identified where you will obtain your data and designed the collection tools?
- When will you collect, analyse and interpret the data?
- How much time do you need to allow for writing up the research project?

This timeline, when added to the research questions, gave Julie a clear structure at the outset of her research. It also helped her feel more secure in the early stages when she found the task ahead very daunting. However, she also remained adaptable and did alter this timeline as events developed. For instance, she continued to add to her literature review throughout the research though much of this was done at the beginning. She also kept in touch with her tutor more closely than the plan indicated and was able to write up earlier parts of the project in draft form before all of the data had been analysed.

Table 4.3   Research timeline for a dissertation project into student learning in HE

Time	Tasks in order	People involved	Time expected to do task
Semester 1. October	Check research questions and plan with dissertation tutor	Dissertation tutor	1 day
October	Obtain permission from head of Education Studies to conduct the research	Head of Education Studies	1 day
October/ January	Undertake a literature search for relevant material	Researcher	4 weeks
Semester 2. January/ February	Design questionnaire for first year education studies students about their learning experiences	Researcher	1 week
January/ February	Design focus group questions for the students	Researcher	2 days
January/ February	Design interview schedule for lecturers	Researcher	2 days
February	Identify module session to give out questionnaires and ask permission from the lecturer	Researcher and lecturer	1 day
February	Identify three lecturers to interview Ask for their consent	Researcher and lecturers	1 day
February	Ask for volunteers to make a focus group from the student body via group email sent by programme administrator Identify those to be involved	Researcher, programme administrator, individual students	3 days
February/ March	Pilot and adjust questionnaire in the light of feedback	Small number of Education Studies student friends	2 days
March (early)	Conduct questionnaire in allocated time during module session	Researcher and students on a chosen module	1 day
March (mid to late)	Conduct focus group	Researcher and small group of students	1 day
March	Conduct interviews with lecturers	Researcher and lecturers	3 days
April (early)	Collate findings from the questionnaires, focus group and interviews	Researcher	1 week
April (mid)	Analyse results using the original research questions and making links with the literature review	Researcher	1 week
April (end)	Tutorial to discuss findings and results	Researcher and tutor	1 day
Begin in mid April to mid May	Writing up of dissertation Ensuring page numbers, headings, bibliography and abstract are completed	Researcher	1 week
Mid to late May	Proof reading of final copy	Researcher and friend	1 day
Late May	Running off copies, ring binding and submission of dissertation	Researcher and tutor	1 day

Research projects can vary greatly. The design chosen will reflect a researcher's ideology of education and research, as noted in previous chapters. It will also be influenced by the nature of the research focus, the respondents, and the resources available to a researcher.

Project evaluations

You may wish to use research methods to monitor and evaluate a specific project that you are implementing. In such cases it is even more important that the planning and timeline are done before the commencement of the project. Below is an initial planning proforma. This was used by a group of teachers introducing and developing curriculum projects as part of a networked learning community, but the same outline can be used to evaluate all kinds of project.

Evaluation focus
In a few sentences outline your aims.

- **List what will be done as part of the project**
  Think of structural changes, spending needed, materials to be developed, actions to be taken by specific people, training needs, specific events, visits, etc.
- **Outcomes**
  What do you hope will be achieved? (Think of pupils, students, trainers, staff, others. Will there be any measures/indicators? Include important outcomes which may not be easy to measure.)
- **How will we know?**
  What methods can be used for seeing/measuring what has been done/the process? Identify how outcomes can be measured/identified. Who will be the respondents? (think of a broad range of methods). (*Later each method of data collection and a timeline can be designed in detail.*)

Figure 4.1   Evaluation planning proforma

Using the planning proforma

Evaluation focus
This section is to outline the project to be evaluated. It is effectively a statement and discussion of aims. These, when linked to the outcomes hoped for, effectively become the research questions of the evaluation.

What will be done in the project
Here the changes that need to/will be put in place to enable the development to take place are listed (e.g. allocation of hours to carry out tasks, rooming and equipment requirements that need to be met, special training requirements

of trainers/teachers/assistants). It will also outline the process that needs to take place, such as changes in the curriculum content, the adaptation of teaching methods, and any special activities that need to be introduced. An example here could be the suspension of the normal timetable to allow pupils to work with a professional dance troupe.

Outcomes

This is a list or discussion of what it is hoped the outcomes of the project will be. These are a clearer statement of how we judge if the aims have been met.

How will we know?

Here the researchers identify from whom data will be collected and the data gathering methods that will be used. In these last two sections the evaluation team will need to consider the significance of different types of data (quantitative and/or qualitative) to their results.

   The discussion by the evaluation/research team members that is required to fill out the proforma serves to clarify what will be done in the project, how it will be done and the data that will show how successful it has been. It also allows us to move on to develop a timeline showing when things will happen and when data will be gathered. This in turn will enable the identification of who will gather the data and analyse it. There is now a clear plan for the project and its evaluation and the researchers are likely to feel more in control of the process. Each project presents unique problems as it unfolds. However, having devised a clear plan at the outset should help the project team cope with changing circumstances.

 Student Activity

Planning a research project

The following activities will form the initial, planning stages of your research project. This plan will be further developed through the tasks at the end of subsequent chapters.

1. Using the appropriate sections of this chapter to guide you:
    (a) identify a research focus;
    (b) construct appropriate research questions;
    (c) write a title for the project.

2. If you belong to a research group, write this initial plan as a PowerPoint and present it to the group for discussion. This will enable you to refine the project in the light of supportive criticism.

3. Use the BERA (http://www.bera.ac.uk/) guidelines for ethical research to examine the research questions that you have written above. Identify any ethical issues to be addressed for each of the questions.

Conclusion

In considering how you can design and embark upon a research project, we have emphasised the importance of developing a clear focus and research questions. It is also important to be organised in terms of scheduling each stage of the research into an appropriate time frame. In Chapter 5 we discuss the significance of published research and other relevant literature to new research projects and consider how it can best be accessed and used.

Recommended Reading

Lewis, I. and Munn, P. (2004) *So You Want to do Research! A Guide for Beginners on How to Formulate Research Questions.* Edinburgh: The Scottish Council for Research in Education. This is one in a series of short practical research guides published by the SCR. It is, as the title suggests, a guide to the writing of research questions for those who are new to research.

Punch, K. (2000) *Developing Effective Research Proposals.* London: Sage. As the title would suggest, this volume takes the reader through the stages of developing a research proposal. As such it is an accessible publication designed for those embarking on the research process.

Silverman, D. (2005) *Doing Qualitative Research* (second edition). London: Sage. This is a very good text for those interested in qualitative approaches to research. It discusses how to design and plan your research project as well as all aspects of conducting qualitative research. Though it primarily refers to PhD research it is still useful for all researchers.

Yates, S. (2004) *Doing Social Science Research.* London: Sage and the Open University Press. This book is useful for those who are new to the research process. Written as a general text for social science students, it provides an introductory overview of the research process. It offers a clear explanation of the main research paradigms and their associated methodologies. Many interesting readings are used as illustrative examples.

5

Accessing and using literature

As researchers get deeper into their project the significance of existing research and relevant literature becomes clear. This chapter discusses the purposes of literature review, how and where to find relevant research or related literature, and how to write it up within a study.

Purposes of literature review

Researchers need to access and review existing research and relevant literature in order to

- provide background information on the general area of study;
- describe and evaluate the context of the research (social, political, economic, educational, environmental, and so on);
- consider and comment on what has already been written within the general area of investigation, looking particularly at the relationships (differences and similarities) between studies;
- discuss the relevance of existing research to the research focus and methodology (including any impact on the intended research questions).

To illustrate these four points, consider the following extracts from a paper the authors wrote on some small-scale research into the performance management of teachers (Burton and Bartlett, 2002).

Teacher education is increasingly conceptualised within an extended framework from initial training, through induction to the NQT year and beyond into qualified teacher status (Heaney, 2001). All teachers are now subject to an annual performance review. Performance management is seen as an ongoing cycle involving planning, monitoring and review (DfEE, 2000b).
(Background information)

The changes also include a 'fast track' through the profession to early subject leadership, senior management roles and on to headship (DfEE, 1999). Top quality graduates and 'the most talented serving teachers' will be selected for their commitment to teaching, excellent subject knowledge, and their talent to communicate, inspire and lead. They will move more quickly through the pay scales and take up senior leadership roles within a few years of joining the teaching profession. The creation of AST (Advanced Skill Teacher) and fast track posts has been highly controversial as the availability of a few highly paid posts militates against a collegial approach to school improvement. Thus the government's policy encourages a restricted view of professional activity with a narrow emphasis on the classroom and the techniques of teaching (Bottery and Wright, 1999). It also serves to fragment and divide groups of teachers who will be differentiated by their 'labels' and their salaries whilst the nature of their professional tasks will be fundamentally the same.
(Describing the context)

The performance management model also promotes a focus on the individual teacher as opposed to the subject or year team, yet we know that much of the creative pedagogic and curriculum development work emanates from a team approach. This focus on individual development, and management by objectives, contrasts with a 'total quality management' model of development which emphasises collaboration and teamwork (Deming, 1986; Scholtes, 1998).
(Commenting on literature on the general area of the research)

The linking of individual performance to pay, rather than increasing the motivation of teachers, may have had the opposite effect, as suggested by the results of a Mori poll conducted after the first round of applications by teachers to cross the performance threshold (Mansell, 2001). Thompson (2000) suggests that teachers are not enthusiastic about individual pay initiatives. Thus a small-scale impact study in which seven teachers from five schools in the North West were interviewed about their perceptions of, and attitudes towards, the performance management processes and threshold assessment payments in their schools, was conducted to address the following research questions:

- How has performance management affected teaching effectiveness and pupil achievement?
- How has achieving threshold status affected teachers as teaching professionals?
(Relevance of existing research to research questions)

Critiquing research studies

As a new researcher it is important that you read other research to gain a greater understanding of what has been already done in your field and also to learn more about the process of research itself (see pp. 60–62 on writing a literature review). This reading is not the totally passive activity that you may at first think and it is important that you develop the ability to critique other work.

In carrying out a critique you need to identify the position that the writers have taken as researchers. In light of this you will be able to examine the methods they used, how these were conducted, the findings and any conclusions they drew. You will then be able to consider the alternative positions that could be taken, other methods that would follow, and how these could alter the nature of the findings. This process of critique will not only develop a greater understanding of research alternatives and findings but will also give you greater insight into your own positioning.

Checklist for carrying out a critique of research

1. Aims and findings

Give a brief outline of the purposes of the research. It may be useful to indicate findings here.

2. Standpoint

Outline the theoretical standpoint taken. This should be compared to other alternatives. It should be related to the purposes of the research (i.e. how the standpoint taken is reflected in the purposes of the research).

3. Data collection

Briefly outline the methods used to collect data. These must be considered in relation to the theoretical standpoint taken. Alternative methods of data collection should be discussed. Their relation to other standpoints may also be assessed.

4. Findings and conclusions

What are the key findings from the research? Are they supported by the data?

5. Strengths

What are the strengths of this piece of research? In discussing these you must consider the theoretical standpoint taken, the methods of data collection chosen and their relationship to the purposes of the research.

6. Weakneses/omissions

In light of the theoretical standpoint and methods chosen what are the weaknesses of this piece of research? This may consider the internal weaknesses of the actual study but also the alternatives that different standpoints would offer.

---

7. Worthiness of the research

Do you think that this research was worthwhile? This is of course a value judgement and you should consider what has been gained from the research. This may be a greater understanding of the phenomena researched, how to carry out research, or how to interpret data. You are effectively considering the contribution this research makes to knowledge in its broadest sense.

Student Activity

Critique of a research article

Choose a research article from a major educational research journal, such as the *British Educational Research Journal* or *Educational Action Research*, that is about an area of education that you are particularly interested in.
   Using the headings from the checklist for carrying out a critique of research, critically reflect upon its design, implementation and findings.
   Consider its implications for your own research interests.

Types of available source material

The extent to which researchers can access a wide range of sources in conducting research projects will depend on how much writing and research they are used to doing and how much time they have available. Generally speaking, if one is looking for the latest research on a particular topic, journal articles are by far the best resource as they publish the most recent findings on highly specific issues. Many journals are also published on-line, making them even easier to access. Books tend to be longer in production and therefore any research referred to tends not to be so current. Books are usually better, however, for providing background information or policy overviews. Official publications such as government papers (for example from DCSF, DIUS, TDA and OFSTED) contain policy and strategy statements which are often essential for researchers to understand the genesis of and motives for certain developments. Documents produced within schools and local authorities can help provide factual and descriptive information to contextualise the research setting; they may also raise issues in relation to the research questions.

   In education the pace of change is fast and developments can sometimes be dramatic, so you will require up-to-date commentary on new policy initiatives and the responses to them from teacher unions. Reputable newspapers such as the *Times Educational Supplement*, *Education Guardian* and *Independent*

Education provide a useful service in this regard, often sourcing their pieces from educational experts. They offer information about developments in particular schools and publish the results from major research studies, such as the Trends in International Mathematics and Science Study (TIMSS) which has compared the mathematics and science achievement of pupils across the world in 1995, 1999, 2003 and 2007. They also cover in detail the latest political and professional debates – and of course it is important to remember that all newspapers have a licence for editorial bias! For certain information, then, newspapers are a credible source to cite as long as they form only a small part of the material accessed.

Conducting a library search

The following guidance is adapted from publications by Jackie Fealey and colleagues of the Liverpool John Moores University learning resource centre. It is applicable to most other library contexts.

A literature search is a systematic search through the many resources outlined below in order to locate information on a given subject. It is essential to define a topic as closely as possible and consider any limits that could be applied, such as date or language of publication. Compiling a list of search terms, i.e. keywords and phrases, acronyms and synonyms, which describe the subject is a good starting point. Using both British and American spellings where appropriate will ensure comprehensive coverage and including narrow and broad terms will enable the search to be narrowed if too much information is found, or to broaden it if the converse is true.

Books
Books in most libraries are arranged according to the Dewey Decimal Classification system. Within this system the subject of Education is classified between the numbers 370–379, although the teaching of a subject above primary level is classified with the subject, for example teaching primary maths is classed at 372.7 (with education), while teaching secondary maths is classed at 510.7 (with mathematics). As well as checking the stock on the shelves, researchers can usually search the library catalogue electronically in a number of ways, including by author, title, keyword, and subject.

Journals
An increasing number of journals are now available electronically across the World Wide Web and titles held in university libraries are listed in their catalogues and on electronic resource pages. Lists of titles held electronically are easily available from any good academic library, and if the institution pays a subscription fee to the publishers researchers can gain access to full text electronic journals. Common search databases include:

- Academic Search Complete: designed specifically for academic institutions, containing more than 5,300 full-text periodicals, including 4,400 peer-reviewed journals. In addition to full text, this database offers indexing and abstracts for more than 9,300 journals and a total of 10,900 publications including monographs, reports, conference proceedings, and so on. The database features PDF content going back as far as 1865, with the majority of full text titles in native (searchable) PDF format.
- Education Research Complete: the definitive online resource for education research. Topics covered include all levels of education from early childhood to higher education, and all the educational specialties, such as multilingual education, health education, and testing. Education Research Complete provides indexing and abstracts for more than 1,840 journals, as well as full text for more than 950 journals, and includes full text for more than 81 books and monographs, and for numerous education-related conference papers.
- InformaWorld: offers full-text access to over 1,000 leading academic journals from the publishers Taylor and Francis, covering over 350,000 articles in the social sciences, arts, humanities, science, medicine and technology.
- ScienceDirect: provides online access to over 2,000 journals published by Elsevier. It is possible to view abstracts or full-text articles, including any photographs, tables or graphics featured in the printed article. The full text collection of over 1 million articles from 1995 to the present covers a variety of subject areas.
- Swetswise: provides online access to the tables of contents of over 18,000 journals and full-text access to articles.

Once connected to an electronic journal service a known article can be selected or all the journals available through that service can be searched by subject, keyword or author's name.

Indexing and abstracting services
Indexing and abstracting services (often known simply as abstracts and indexes) are used to locate journal articles on particular subjects or by particular authors. They are published regularly (usually weekly, monthly or quarterly) and provide a means of keeping track of the thousands of journal articles that appear each year. The layout of each publication varies, but each service will provide sufficient information to enable researchers to locate the article in a library. Journals cited should be checked against the catalogue to see if they are held in the library or online. The following on-line service provides references to journal articles in Education.

- British Education Index: this has three sections – the Australian Education Index, the British Education Index and ERIC, the American Education Index. The service can be linked through the library system to provide links to the full-text documents.
- Web of Science: this is part of ISI Web of Knowledge, an integrated platform designed to support research. Web of Science includes the Science

Citation Index (covering over 5,000 major scientific journals), the Social Sciences Citation Index (covering 1,700 core social science journals) and the Arts and Humanities Citation index (covering over 1,000 arts and humanities journals) from 1981 to the present.
- 'Alert Systems' allow researchers to keep up to date with relevant new articles and papers in their chosen subject areas. ZETOC, the British Library alerting system, provides access to the British Library's Electronic Table of Contents of around 20,000 current journals and around 16,000 conference proceedings published per year. The database covers 1993 to the present and is updated on a daily basis, also providing link for full-text access.

Athens DA Username and password are required to access these services.

Dissertations (Theses)
Most academic libraries have collections of students' dissertations produced as part of higher degree courses, such as MSc, MPhil, or PhD. These can usually be referred to within the library but cannot be taken away or copied.
   Dissertations are indexed in:

- British National Bibliography for report literature (1998 – the present);
- Index to Theses (ASLIB): an electronic version is available via the Electronic Journals and Datasets page.

Reports
Reports are issued mostly by research establishments, the government, or private industry and are usually practical, up-to-date and detailed. Libraries will have a selection of reports. Note that education reports are classified according to the subject of the report.

Newspapers
Newspapers can be very useful sources of contemporary reports and comment on new legislation and events. Libraries will take a number of newspapers including daily broadsheets and the weekly education newspapers, the *Times Educational Supplement* and the *Times Higher Education Supplement*, back copies of which are available on microfilm. Usually these cover from about the mid-seventies to the mid-nineties, and thereafter can be found on CD-ROM and online. Alternatively there are electronic newspapers' direct links available:

- Factiva: provides a global news information service providing access to over 1700 newspapers from around the world;
- Times Digital Archive: access to a complete archive from 1785–1985.

The World Wide Web

The volume of information available via the internet is expanding daily and can provide an additional, if sometimes overwhelming, resource. It is best to search via a university library subject information page as this will have links to relevant sites such as the DCSF, DIUS, NFER, Learndirect, and the like, as well as electronic journals, special education sites, research bodies, publishers and lots of sites supporting different curriculum subjects. However, researchers can strike out on their own by choosing one of the many search engines available and doing a keyword search of the whole. Caution is urged here as large amounts of information, often of dubious quality, will undoubtedly deluge the novice searcher.

Recording references

As your search progresses it is worth keeping details of any potentially useful items you encounter. If you do this accurately and consistently, you can refer back to useful material as your research develops. It also makes compiling the reference list, which should always appear at the end of the study, an easy task. A reference should always include the following basic information: who wrote the item, its year of publication, its title and who published it. It may also be useful to include the place of publication. There are several ways of presenting this information. We recommend that you adopt the Harvard style and record references to books as follows:

Bell, J. (2005) *Doing Your Research Project: A Guide for First-Time Researchers in Education, Health and Social Science* (fourth edition). Maidenhead: Open University Press.

and references to journal articles as follows:

Kraft, N. (2002) 'Teacher research as a way to engage in critical reflection: a case study', *Reflective Practice,* 3(2): 175–190.

 Student Activity

Comparing published educational research

Read any copy of both the *British Educational Research Journal* and the *Educational Action Research Journal* since the year 2005. Compare their approaches in terms of:

- the focus of the editorials;
- the positioning of the different articles published in each of the journals;
- the range of research methodologies;
- the scope of articles.

Writing literature reviews

If you are going on to present your work for an award-bearing course or publish it in a journal or book, your whole study will need to be written up in a structured way. Many texts in our reference lists provide guidance on doing this and we deal with it ourselves in Chapter 11. What follows here is some specific advice on writing literature reviews.

A literature review should convey an overview of the knowledge and ideas that have already been established on a topic and what their strengths and weaknesses are (Taylor & Proctor, 2001). Its guiding concept will be the research objective of the study for which the review has been undertaken. It should identify areas of controversy in the literature and formulate questions that need further research. It is also important to provide as balanced a view of competing perspectives as possible (within the limits of your inevitable proclivity for a particular stance). The Evidence for Policy and Practice Information and Co-ordinating Centre (EPPI-Centre, 2003) produces 'systematic reviews' which aim to find as much as possible of the research relevant to particular research questions, and use explicit methods to identify what can reliably be said on the basis of these studies. Such reviews then go on to synthesise research findings in an easily accessible form which reduces the bias inherent in less rigorous approaches to review. Whilst you may find the outputs from these systematic reviews helpful the approach is not one you could emulate since the process is very labour-intensive and time consuming. Remember, it is neither possible nor desirable to review everything; your aim is to find the studies that are of most relevance to your intended project and to isolate within each study the methodology and findings together with any underlying concepts, arguments or theories. You should then consider the implications of and relationships between these findings and suggestions in the context of your own focus of investigation. If writing up the project for a dissertation or article, you will need to refer back to the significant literature within your discussion of the research findings in order to highlight any relationships between the new and existing research.

It may be helpful initially in writing up a literature review for you to use a key overview text to describe the general area of study, or 'map the terrain'. You can then supplement this by drawing on related books, chapters, journals articles or news cuttings to develop the main structure of your argument and to support, add to or put a different slant on particular points. The basic approach here is to start with the general and become ever more specific and precise as you home in on your research focus. It is always best to access the most up-to-date sources available, as these should refer to any seminal work from the past as well as dealing with the latest research or policy developments.

Knowing when to use direct quotes from the literature is a skill that can be developed by reading existing reviews and papers. Generally, it is best to keep direct quotes to a minimum, and to attempt instead to weave an author's point into your own argument or to indicate support for a point you are making by adding the author's name and date of relevant publication in brackets after that point. Direct quotes should only be used when the meaning needs to be unadulterated for maximum impact. The author's name, date of publication and the page number of the quote should always be cited in the text, with the relevant reference included in the bibliography or reference list. The quote will then need to be commented upon in order to justify its use and to retain the flow of the argument.

Sometimes it is easy to be drawn deeper and deeper into reading and to fail to get down to any writing, so you need to be disciplined enough to take frequent notes that will summarise at intervals what the literature is saying in relation to your proposed new research. Reviewing literature is best done by writing this in your own words, organising your notes around embryonic key arguments or points of enquiry. As the piece develops your structure will be critically important – using key headings, each with their own sub-headings or arguments, will help to draw out the relationships between issues and findings systematically. The example shown below shows how this structure might work.

There is a great deal of current interest in learning styles and many teachers have embarked on research studies in this field. The following example is an outline plan of what might be included in a fairly extensive review of learning styles research and literature.

Example: Outline plan for reviewing learning styles literature

- *Intro*
  Learning styles literature is extensive, varied, and based on several different research approaches: 'We will look at four distinct approaches and their respective research findings/researchers' positions … '
- *Key Heading 1 – Learning Styles*
  Subheadings: Definition of learning style construct; Imager/Verbaliser; Holist/Serialist; Field-dependent/Field-Independent; Visual/Auditory/Kinaesthetic; Relationships between categorisations; Implications for the classroom.
- *Key Heading 2 – Learning Strategies*
  Subheadings: Definition of learning strategy construct; Experiential learning – its characteristics; Kolb's Cycle; Application to learners.
- *Key Heading 3 – Learning Approaches*
  Subheadings: Definition of learning approaches construct; Motives for learning; Deep/Surface learning; Approaches nurtured within UK classrooms/lectures.
- *Key Heading 4 – Learning Preferences*
  Subheadings: Definition of learning preferences construct; Attitudinal and physical preferences; Learning Preferences Inventory; Relevance to different ages and stages of learners.
- *Conclusion*
  Summarise key features of the four different approaches; suggest the relative relevance of each to the context of the research; discuss potential application of one approach to the research project, indicating the research questions it implies.

Student Activity

Beginning a literature search

Use the focus decided upon when you completed the tasks for Chapter 4 to begin a literature search. List a number of literature sources that:

- provide background information on the general area of study;
- describe and evaluate the context of the research;
- consider and comment on what has already been written within the general area of investigation;
- discuss the existing research that is relevant to the research focus and methodology.

Conclusion

We have seen how accessing previous research studies and relevant literature is essential to the development and refinement of a research project. Reviewing the significant findings of other researchers not only helps to establish a sound platform for further research questions within a project but also plays a part in extending the body of research in an area. In this way, education researchers can act as a community to share and improve their understanding of a wide range of issues. In reviewing and commenting upon government reports or official policy documents researchers are able to outline and evaluate the policy issues germane to their research. Such literature, along with the relevant institutional reports such as curriculum documentation, can contribute to the communication of a context for the project. Engaging with the literature is a fundamental part of the process by which researchers will construct, review and reconstruct their views and questions about particular educational practices and their wider implications.

In Chapter 6 we turn to a consideration of case studies and experiments as strategies that researchers may employ in their studies.

Recommended Reading

Hart, C. (2001) *Doing a Literature Search*. London: Sage. This is a comprehensive guide to planning and conducting a literature search. It explains how to find appropriate books, articles, official publications and statistics on a chosen research focus.

Woods, P. (2006) *Successful Writing for Qualitative Researchers*. London: Routledge. This book considers all aspects of the writing up process. Even if you are not aiming for wider publication, you may find it useful to review the sections on organising work, style and format, editing and collaborative writing. This is a useful text to read before commencing your final writing up.

6

Research strategies: case studies and experiments

This chapter outlines the case study approach, which is a very popular strategy with education researchers. It also considers the use of experiments which, though in their purest form are only possible in highly controlled conditions, may be adapted to meet the needs of education research.

Case studies

The case study approach is not a method as such, but a research strategy where the researcher aims to study one case in depth. Work in the legal and medical professions is very much based upon case studies (see Hammersley et al., 2000 and Silverman, 2005, for a discussion of the use of cases in varying contexts). Here particular cases are examined, usually in order to produce a solution or cure to the issue in question. Each case is unique, which is what makes them so interesting, however, the professionals involved are able to draw upon their knowledge of previous similar cases in order to understand the one currently being examined and to help them decide upon an appropriate ruling or action. For instance, since the law recently allowed parents to be prosecuted for truancy the first test case which resulted in a mother being imprisoned has provided case law for similar prosecutions to be tested against.

Thus case law is built up in the courts and develops a body of understanding about a set of issues. Medical knowledge is similarly built up through a series of practical cases. Education research can also use a case study approach to develop understanding within a range of settings. There are many examples of where case studies have been used in education research to illustrate particular theoretical arguments. Seminal case studies include Ball's (1981) 'Beachside Comprehensive' and Lacey's (1970) 'Hightown Grammar'.

Education professionals can draw upon their own experience and documented accounts of previous cases to help them analyse, explain and, where appropriate, suggest action. Their own findings can in turn be added to a growing body of case histories. This is a popular strategy in education research, where using a case study approach can enable professionals to research important aspects of their own working environment without being forced to collect large representative samples from a national frame. What actually constitutes a case is defined by the researcher and can vary enormously in size. Thus the case could be a local authority, a youth club, a class, or a particular individual.

By concentrating on a particular case or cases, data are usually collected by using several methods. Thus researchers will investigate sites of practice that they may have existing knowledge of (e.g. teachers could investigate their own classrooms). Likewise students of Education Studies may use their work placements or perhaps return to their previous schools, using this knowledge as a starting point, producing a descriptive account to set the scene. They may then observe in a more detached way, treating the case as anthropologically strange. Other data are typically collected from documents, records, photographs and interviews. Anderson (1998) suggests that most case study research in education is interpretive seeking to bring a case to life. He states that they often, but not exclusively, occur in a natural setting with the researcher employing qualitative and/or quantitative methods and measures as befit the circumstances. As Yin (2009) notes, the forms that the data collected will take essentially depend upon the nature of the particular case to be investigated.

In this way triangulation automatically takes place, thereby increasing the validity of the study. The consideration of data in case studies can also involve fellow students who might be studying the same phenomenon in a different setting. As such, you might comment upon and discuss the research in light of your different experiences. In action research, case studies are felt to be more valid as a result of such peer scrutiny. Case studies investigated by practising professionals, such as teachers, youth workers and community development officers, are generally acknowledged to contribute to their own professional development.

A major criticism of case studies is that they lack a representativeness of the wider population and thus researchers are unable to make generalisations from their findings. However, proponents would claim that the importance of the case study approach comes via the in-depth analysis and the understanding gained. For these researchers, the strength of this research approach lies in the 'relatability' of the findings (Bassey, 1990). By this term, Bassey is suggesting that while each case may be unique there will be sufficient similarities to make the findings from one study useful when seeking to understand others.

Three examples of case studies which could be carried out equally well by people who worked in the environment studied, or by visiting researchers such as students, are described below. The cases chosen are of different sizes and each occurs within a different setting. The first looks at the implementation of an integrated curriculum approach at Key Stage One in a primary school. Here, one key stage in the school is the case. The second example is of a Year 2 class of 35 pupils visiting a farm, whilst the third involves the teaching of citizenship in a secondary school. The strength of such a research approach is that the researchers are using a range of research methods in order to investigate a particular issue. It is important to remain cognisant of the very small-scale nature of these particular studies. We should be very loathe to make over-elaborate claims for the findings from such cases.

Examples of cases

Case study: Example 1: Summary

 Title

An evaluation of the introduction of an integrated curriculum in one primary school at Key Stage 1.

Initial research questions

1. Why was an integrated curriculum being introduced?
2. How was this implemented?
3. What have been the effects of the introduction of the integrated curriculum on pupils' learning?

Methods of data collection

Interviews with a sample of teachers.
Questionnaire administered to a class of pupils.
Three pupil focus groups.
Researcher diary.
Lesson observations.
Analysis of examples of pupil work.

Findings

Pupils enjoyed the opportunity to work on topics that allowed them to explore their interests more. Whilst being aware of the difficulties of introducing a more integrated curriculum approach, staff commented that it maintained the children's motivation and they were much more able to use their own intiative. The teachers felt the new approach offered them more flexibility in their teaching and enabled pupils to develop their creative skills to greater effect.

Description of case study 1

The school identified a need to develop creativity in the curriculum. The teachers realised that the National Curriculum (NC) and how they delivered it in subject slots throughout the school day was restricting, in that it limited the scope for both pupils and teachers to be adaptable in their learning. They also felt that pupils were losing motivation when following a subject-based curriculum. It was proposed to make a more integrated curriculum where the NC was delivered via a topic approach.

In this approach a topic, theme, or issue is studied, such as 'Houses and Homes'. The teacher designs a topic web whereby key areas are explored in the lessons by the pupils. In this way different aspects of the various curriculum subjects, such as maths, English, geography, science and history, are covered.

The advantages of this approach are that the learning is about the particular topic or focus and the different subject knowledge is approached holistically rather than being broken into separate and distinct areas. It remains relevant to the learners who can see its applicability rather than being disjointed and lacking in relevance to them as can be the case when subjects are taught as discrete units. The teachers hoped that organising the curriculum in this way would enable the development of increasingly individualised learning and encourage greater questioning and exploration by the pupils, thus allowing for greater creativity.

This particular research was conducted by a teacher at the school as part of his dissertation, but it could be conducted by any researcher who could gain permission from the school and was able to spend a period of time collecting data. The amount of data collected will depend significantly upon the time allocated by the researcher to be spent in the school.

The integrated curriculum was introduced in the school in the autumn term and the data collection took place in the following summer term. The researcher wanted to know if this curriculum did motivate pupils and allow them to explore further and become more creative. In order to do this he needed to gather data from both pupils and their teachers. To make the research more manageable he decided to just look at Key Stage 1. He looked at the work the pupils had produced over the year, interviewed six teachers, gave all pupils in the key stage a suitably designed questionnaire, and held three pupil focus groups of eight pupils in each. He also kept a diary of classroom activities between Easter and June.

Findings

The teachers commented that they had specific concerns when the curriculum was being introduced about the extra work involved in planning this whole new approach. They also had other concerns about adopting a completely different way of working. Whilst they would have liked more support during its launch, and did at times feel very isolated, they believed that the scheme would help to maintain the children's interest and motivation in lessons and that they would be much more able to use their intiative. The teachers also felt it would offer them more flexibility in their teaching. Though rather unsure at first when the clear subject guidelines of the NC were abandoned, they were now finding this freedom to explore issues with the pupils more rewarding. Though there was as yet no clear evidence in terms of assessment results, they felt that the quality of the pupil learning was better with this 'deeper' integrated approach.

In the questionnaires, and also during the focus groups, the pupils were able to describe the things they had done in class. They had enjoyed working on topics and the investigations and problem solving involved. What became apparent from talking to the pupils and also by looking at their work was the personalisation of learning that an integrated curriculum allowed, with pupils working on different aspects of a topic and at different levels of difficulty. It was apparent that pupils were motivated to do more and more, rather than just complete particular pieces of set work.

There were criticisms of this approach, in that some teachers pointed to the need to ensure that all the important areas of the subject curriculum were covered. It was also said that it was not necessarily the subject curriculum itself that led to a lack of pupil motivation, but the way in which it was linked to assessment and the pressures in school that this caused. It was interesting that some of the more experienced teachers commented that this was not really a new approach as this was how they had taught when they had begun in the profession, long before the introduction of the National Curriculum.

The researcher concluded that the integrated curriculum had been generally well introduced, but that for such large-scale changes there needed to be support for the teachers introducing it and continued evaluation. He felt that there needed to be continuous monitoring to ensure that the initial momentum was maintained and would hope to see more lesson observation and data collection by all the teachers involved as the curriculum moved into its second year. It will be interesting to monitor the NC assessment results for this school over the next few years.

Commentary

This is an interesting case study carried out by a teacher in his own school. It has a number of benefits in terms of developing the research skills of the teacher and involving other members of staff. It promoted discussion and raised awarenes which ultimately led to changes in practice. We should also, however, be mindful if its limitations. This study is of one school only and while this may be relatable to others it is not possible to make generalisations from just this single case. Whilst researching the place in which he worked meant he had valuable knowledge of the school, it also could mean he was blinkered to curriculum approaches used in other schools which may have affected how he saw and reported things. The fact that the staff knew the researcher well may have affected their honesty about how effective the National Curriculum had been.

Case study: Example 2: Summary

 Title

A day visit to a working farm museum: an evaluation of a curriculum event.

Research questions

1. What did the pupils do on their day visit?
2. How did the activities and learning on the visit relate to the school curriculum?
3. What did pupils and staff think of the experience?

Methods of data collection

Interviews with teachers and adult helpers.
Pupils' written accounts.
Focus groups of pupils.
Analysis of pre- and post-work by pupils.

Findings

The visit did cover various aspects of the NC, particularly science, geography, history and English. The pupils, teachers and helpers all really enjoyed the day and the benefits in terms of building relationships seem to be at least as important as the actual formal curriculum gains.

Description of Case Study 2

This piece of research was of a day visit by 35 Year 2 pupils, one teacher, three teaching assistants and five parent helpers to a working farm museum in the Midlands. It took place on a warm sunny day in early June. The pupils had been preparing for the visit in advance by exploring aspects of science, history and geography. They had been studying the National Curriculum science topics 'Life Processes and Living Things', 'Humans and other Animals' and 'Living Things in their Environment'. They had also learned about how people lived and earned their living in the past in rural communities and how food is produced through farming.

The journey to the farm took about 45 minutes on the coach and when they arrived the pupils were put into seven pre-arranged groups of five that they were to work in throughout the day. Everyone had a workbook, written for this age group of pupils and supplied by the farm museum. Each group started at a different part of the site and worked their way around the map and workbook. This avoided them all grouping together in any one part of the farm and becoming too crowded. There were different activities and demonstrations timetabled to take place at various times throughout the day, and the adults with each group were aware of these and factored them into their route to ensure that the children saw them all. These involved feeding different animals, weaving, basket making, butter making, and working the forge. In each area there were also activities for the children to take part in. Everyone came together in a picnic area for lunch and met at the farm shop at the end of the day.

On the day itself the researcher was not assigned to one group of pupils alone but went from one to another spending time with each, witnessing all of the timetabled activities. She made notes on the pupil involvement in the activities, how the children were filling in the worksheets or not, and on the general interactions taking place between children and adults. The researcher also took pictures of the pupils working during the day. These were for research purposes but it had been agreed they were also to be used by the school in a display about the visit. (It should be noted that there was an agreement with parents for photographs to be taken as part of school activities and these were all to be given to the school to use and not to be kept after the analysis by the researcher.) Two days after the visit the researcher interviewed the teacher, the three teaching assistants and two of the parent helpers. Data were collected from a whole class discussion and the pupils also wrote their own views on the visit as part of a writing activity. Pupils' preparation work before and after the visit was also analysed by the researcher.

Findings

The researcher found that the teacher had visited this working farm before and this had now become an annual school trip that was looked forward to by the pupils. The teacher's prior knowledge meant that she had already identified and prepared work that could be done beforehand in preparation and also afterwards as a follow-up.

The worksheets provided by the farm consisted of a series of tasks and questions for the pupils to work through. However, after the first hour a number of children and adults had given up doing them. Whether they were completed or hardly touched depended upon which group of five the children were in.

The children were interested in all aspects of the farm. They found being near the live animals particularly exciting. Some of the written displays on the farming year and some of the explanations given by the 'actors' they found rather hard to follow. They were very interested in the farm labourer's cottage and what was inside it.

The children did enjoy the day as was evidenced in their written accounts. It was noticeable how they mentioned much more than the actual working farm. For instance, several mentioned the coach trip, who they sat by, the games played at lunchtime, who was in their group of five. This indicates the wide-ranging aspects of the children's experiences during the day. The teacher said that she also enjoyed the day because it enabled her to work with the children outside of the usual classroom setting. She was also aware of how much the children had looked forward to this visit. The teaching assistants echoed these sentiments as well. The parent helpers said how they enjoyed the opportunity to both go to the farm museum and also to be with their children and see how they related to their friends and teachers. The researcher concluded that, whilst the day trip was useful in its goal of covering aspects of the National Curriculum subject content, there are also significant social gains to taking part in such an activity.

Commentary

This case study research was undertaken by a student who was not associated with the school trip but was studying the nature of 'incidental learning' for her final year dissertation. The richness of the findings in such cases is clearly a product of using a range of data collection methods which incorporated both written and oral accounts and elicited both views and opinions as well as factual information from a wide range of participants. Whilst observing our usual cautionary notes about the limitations of using one case, this study does indicate the clear potential of case study methods in examining macro issues, such as incidental learning, which are of interest beyond the school.

Case study: Example 3: Summary

 Title

The teaching of citizenship in a secondary school in the North West of England.

Research questions

1. What is the school policy on the teaching of citizenship?
2. How is citizenship taught in the school?
3. What are the views of

   - pupils
   - teachers

   on the citizenship curriculum?

Methods of data collection

Analysis of official school policy and curriculum documentation.
Analysis of pupil work.
Questionnaire of pupil experiences and opinions.
Focus group interviews with pupils.
Interviews with teachers.

Findings

Citizenship education in its broadest sense takes place in many areas of the curriculum.

Pupils remain largely unaware of the existence of citizenship education as such. Their feelings towards politics are very mixed.

The teachers generally consider the content of citizenship to be very important but are primarily concerned with their subject teaching.

Description of Case Study 3

This piece of research was conducted by an undergraduate Education Studies student for her dissertation. She had an interest in citizenship and political literacy from an earlier module and decided that this would be the focus of her dissertation. She wanted to explore the teaching of citizenship in secondary schools and pupil and teacher attitudes towards it. She had written a literature review that covered different perceptions of citizenship, the development of citizenship in the current political climate, and changes and innovations in the National Curriculum. She now wished to look at the teaching of citizenship in one secondary school as a case study.

The student wrote to the head teacher of the school, someone she knew from her days as a pupil, to gain permission to conduct the research. She was invited to visit to meet the head of Personal Social and Health Education (PSHE) and to set up the data collection. The student arranged several visits during which she showed her questionnaire to the head for approval, arranged to conduct the questionnaire with a tutor group of Year 9 pupils, and set up and conducted a focus group with five pupils from Year 10. She was able to conduct short interviews with the head of PSHE and two other teachers who were form tutors for Year 9. She was also given school policy documents relating to citizenship and PSHE, schemes of work, lesson plans and pupil display work.

Findings

The student accepted that this was a very small-scale case study but that some interesting points had still emerged from the data. The school had a clear policy on the importance of citizenship which states that it was taught across the curriculum when appropriate and also in PSHE lessons. Citizenship clearly appeared at different times in the PSHE curriculum. In the questionnaire she found that the pupils did come across many aspects of the citizenship curriculum but were not necessarily aware of the title. They also did discuss many social issues and concepts, such as fairness, equality and human rights, in a number of subject areas. However, when asked about politics the majority maintained that they had little interest in it and that it was boring. Yet the researcher concluded that they were interested in what was going on around them, that it was the term 'politics' and its image that they objected to. These findings were borne out in the focus group where the pupils did show an interest in local, national and international affairs. They were very aware of issues of social justice but still denied an interest in politics.

The PSHE teacher clearly saw the importance of citizenship and explained where it appeared in the curriculum and gave examples of where citizenship arose in science, history and geography. He did say that he was not sure whether it was called citizenship when covered in these subjects. The science teacher said that he did cover aspects of the quality of life related to citizenship. He saw these as interesting questions but that pupils really needed to understand the science before they could be discussed. The history teacher felt that citizenship was an integral part of history and that it was not really necessary to highlight this.

Thus the researcher concluded that citizenship is taught but that it is often not called this. Also the detail in which the issues are covered varies from teacher to teacher. The researcher would have liked to extend the study to get the views of a wider range of teachers and in addition to have looked at lessons over a period of time.

Commentary

This case is interesting because it enabled the researcher to collect data that reflected some of the points she had noted in her literature review. It demonstrates well how such research can lead to a desire to find out more about what other researchers have explored and about issues of current significance within education communities.

 Student Activity

Outlining cases

Identify two suitable cases that you could research, such as two student friends, two educational institutions that you know, or two academic subjects or options that you are studying.

Write one list that shows similarities and another that identifies the differences between them.

Write a 500-word account that describes and compares the two cases.

The experimental approach

The experimental method is often associated with positivist research (see Chapter 2). Procedures often involve the use of identical experimental and control groups that are kept separate. Whilst the control group is kept constant, specific variables affecting the experimental group are changed in particular ways and the subsequent developments are noted. Any resulting differences between the two groups can be assumed to be due to the changes made to the experimental group. Thus the effects of these variables on the subjects have been 'proved' experimentally. It should be possible to test the findings by replicating the experiment and obtaining the same results.

Experiments are a very useful way of carrying out research in the natural sciences. It is also possible to devise experiments with the participants unwitting throughout. Thus psychologists may design experiments about certain aspects of learning or perception. However, it is difficult to consider whole classroom situations as becoming part of a traditional type of scientific experiment as there are so many variables involved that cannot be kept constant. The individual and unique nature of the human personality militates against the effective designation of control and experimental groups unless one uses very generalised characteristics such as age or gender. Teachers may be able to discern certain characteristics among particular age groups year upon year, however the individuals who make up these teaching groups will not be the same and they may also be very different to teach. In addition, there are important ethical concerns that will arise from setting up experimental and control groups for experiments where classes and groups of children are concerned (see our discussion of ethics in Chapter 3). Thus, in the social sciences, experiments will often take a very different form to those in the natural sciences.

A group of researchers at Birmingham University, concerned with charting and improving classroom behaviour in the 1980s, advocated an experimental approach (Wheldall and Merrett, 1985). Instead of having a control group, their experiments established a baseline of behaviour through an independent observer (a teaching assistant, student visitor, or trainee teacher perhaps) recording aspects of pupil behaviour on an observation schedule. This is done at timed intervals and might, for example, show the number of occasions a particular pupil shouts out in a lesson or gets up from his seat. The teacher then introduces an intervention strategy designed to reduce the pupil's off-task behaviour. This is usually based on the provision of a reward such as credits or verbal praise. The observation is repeated after a period of intervention and the new data are shared with the pupil. This is a straightforward research experiment and easy to implement if another adult is available. What is particularly interesting is whether any improvements in behaviour are sustained over time. This can be achieved by conducting a further observation at some distance in time from the intervention. In cases where rewards are used that are extrinsic to the learner, such as points, credits, or even chocolates and school trips, it is often the case that the benefits are short lived. However, if such rewards are linked to intrinsic rewards, such as better learning or feelings of increased self-worth, the benefits are more likely to be sustained. Student researchers could trial both approaches with different groups, or the same groups in different subjects, to test out this theory.

Student Activity

Designing an experiment

1. Consider a research issue that you could explore via an experiment, e.g. the relationship between attendance at peer-led assignment discussions and assessment outcomes.
2. Outline a specific research question that the experiment would seek to answer, e.g. does the provision of voluntary, peer-led discussion on assignments improve student results?
3. Design a data collection instrument for the experiment, e.g. a chart to show the module results for the last three times the module has run (two before the peer-led sessions were instituted and one after).
4. Analyse and compare the results for before and after the introduction of peer-led assignment discussions as part of the module programme. Carefully consider any reasons for your findings.

Conclusion

The examples referred to in this chapter should provide some ideas about how case studies and experiments might be used within education research projects. As has been shown, the researcher must be alert to both the potential of such strategies to elicit data of interest to the project as well as their shortcomings. In reviewing what has been learned from these examples, researchers might be encouraged to adapt such approaches to their own studies.

In the next two chapters we take a look at two quintessential research methods – questionnaires and interviews.

Recommended Reading

Gomm, R., Hammersley, M. and Forester, P. (eds) (2000) *Case Study Method: Key Issues, Key Texts*. London: Sage. The editors have brought together a number of significant articles that critically discuss the case study approach. This text is for the advanced practitioner researcher who wishes to read further about case studies as a research strategy.

Yin, R. (2009) *Case Study Research: Design and Methods* (Fourth edition). Thousand Oaks, CA: Sage. This updated fourth edition provides a comprehensive guide to case study research. It discusses the importance of the case study as a research strategy and goes on to consider the practicalities of design, collecting evidence, analysis of data and reporting. This is a useful aid to education researchers considering a case study approach.

7

Questionnaires

> This chapter considers the use questionnaires as a method of gathering data. We outline how to design and conduct them and discuss the issues involved in using these techniques by reference to a range of examples.

Questionnaires

When those new to, or unfamiliar with, the research process begin to think of gathering data from groups of people for research purposes, questionnaires are perhaps the method that immediately springs to mind. Pupils faced with a multitude of project assignments are a good example of this as they will invariably resort to data collected via questionnaires. Parents, brothers, sisters and classmates are all potential respondents to a series of questions designed to generate evidence covering a wide range of subjects, such as tastes in clothing, food, leisure activities, music, and so on. A questionnaire is simply a list of questions that respondents can answer. It is clearly a useful method, if carefully planned, for gathering responses from a large number of people relatively quickly. As such, questionnaires may be seen as a useful way of obtaining quantitative data.

Data collected by pupils will produce the sort of evidence that enables the construction of displays including charts and other graphical presentation. However, many teachers who have worked with pupils on designing and conducting questionnaires will doubtless be aware that a questionnaire which yields useful information is not as easy to design as one may think. A well-designed questionnaire can provide useful information on respondents' attitudes, values and habits. However, as is often the case with questionnaires designed by the inexperienced, the information gathered may not be exactly what the researcher is looking for. It is more difficult to obtain in-depth personal responses by this method and both questions and answers will often remain superficial. It is because of this that qualitative researchers find questionnaires less useful. The danger for an inexperienced researcher is in reading an opinion into the data that is not substantiated by the questions. For example, a politician who asks 'How do you rate our taxation policy on a scale of 1 (low) to 5 (high)?' may infer from an average response of 3 that the public are happy with the policy. However, respondents may actually have specific issues with the policy which the question does not allow them to express so as a result they will plump for a nondescript response rating. This example might just as easily be related to school cooks asking pupils to rate school lunches. Certainly your skills as a researcher are important when collecting data by questionnaire. Specific points will need your careful consideration.

Questionnaire design: key points to consider

The design of a questionnaire and the wording of its questions are crucial to its success. Corbetta (2003) points out that the formulation of a questionnaire is a difficult task with no set of formalised precise rules for a researcher to follow. He does suggest however that any researcher needs to begin with a clear research hypothesis or focus and a knowledge of the population who will complete the questionnaire.

(a) Reasons for using a questionnaire

Researchers need to be clear about why they are planning to use a questionnaire to gather data. Whether this is an appropriate method or not will depend upon the type of information that needs to be collected to answer the research questions and the respondents it is going to be collected from. Questionnaires are useful in collecting a large amount of general data and opinions from a large number of people. However, they are of far less use if as a researcher you are collecting detailed information with subtle differences from respondent to respondent. Questionnaires tend to illicit responses that fit into broad categories, with little opportunity for respondents to express complex emotional feelings in response to impersonal questions.

(b) Framing questions

1. It is important for you to be clear about what information you need from the questionnaire and to ask questions which will yield the appropriate data.
2. Each question should have a purpose. Asking questions that are not needed is a waste of your time and resources.
3. Questions need to be specific and your wording should be clear. Appropriate wording for the respondent group should be used, so your wording of questions addressing Year 5 pupils about their experiences of the curriculum is likely to be different from your questionnaire asking for teachers' responses.
4. You must decide the type of question, e.g. you may want to ask pre-coded questions that offer a specific number of responses for the respondent to choose from. For instance, you could ask respondents to tick the choice which best describes their approach to teaching RE, offering them descriptors such as 'multi-faith', 'Anglo-centric', 'spiritual', 'humanist', and so on. Note that pre-coded questions are useful when it comes to collating the answers as they will all fall into one of a set number of categories. However, you need to

consider how appropriate it is to only offer respondents such a limited range of prescribed categories. Questions of this sort may begin to distort the data collected as respondents have to pick a category which is closest to how they would have answered if given a 'free' choice. For this reason you may wish to ask open-ended questions where the respondent can answer in their own words. These are useful in allowing a varied response. However, a wide variation of response makes these questions more difficult to collate. They also involve more commitment to filling in the questionnaire from the respondent and one danger is that respondents will give very brief answers just to finish the questionnaire. Thus remember that asking a large number of open-ended questions may tend to put the respondents off and there by affect the quantity and quality of the data obtained.

5. In many questionnaires the names of respondents will not be asked for, partly to ensure the anonymity of respondents and partly because the sample size is so large that individual responses do not need to be identified. Preserving the anonymity of your respondents needs to be considered very carefully. It may be that it would be useful to follow up respondents that have answered in a certain way later. Therefore offering them anonymity of response would rule this out.

(c) Collecting responses from questionnaires

Though you may want to collect data as a vital part of your research, many of your respondents may not share this interest and so will not be committed to completing the questionnaire. Traditionally many market research surveys are sent out by post. However, these have a notoriously low response rate. In education there is so much information sent through the mail that there is a tendency to deal only with those requiring urgent action and to 'file' the rest, sometimes in a nearby bin! In order to obtain as high a response rate as possible it is useful if you can arrange to distribute and collect responses as this enables you to 'chivvy along' late responses. It is important to distribute at least twice as many questionnaires as you need. This will allow for a level of non-response and in the unlikely event that 100 per cent are returned then so much the better.

All researchers need to have thought out a clear strategy in order to ensure a high return rate of questionnaires. Thus if questionnaires are being distributed to all of the staff of a primary school, for example, it may be best for a researcher to arrange to collect completed questionnaires at the end of the day in person. This can be done without looking at individual responses and thus maintains respondent anonymity. However, in this case the researcher will be aware of who has not yet returned a questionnaire and so can arrange follow-up approaches over subsequent days. However, if staff have been asked to put completed questionnaires in a pigeonhole or a collection tray there is more likely to be a disappointingly low response. The researcher will need to resort to generalised appeals in staff meetings to an unidentified group of non-returners. It is worth reflecting on the efforts taken to ensure that the national census form, for which compulsory completion is backed by the force of law, are all collected in. This is done by a series of checks by the collection team whilst maintaining the confidentiality of respondents' answers.

Questionnaire distribution to pupils can be a much more straightforward process if carefully planned. After all, pupils present a 'captive audience' to researchers. Questionnaires can be given to whole groups of pupils at specific times, such as the beginning or ending of lessons, or during tutor periods, and can be collected in after they have been completed. Another useful point here is that you as the researcher can explain any general points to a class before they start and can answer specific individual questions during the filling in. In this way you could collect information from whole tutor or teaching groups in periods of just 25 to 30 minutes. If collected daily you could have responses from whole year groups by visiting a different tutor group per day for five or six days.

With questionnaires, you must assume that the respondent has answered the questions in good faith. By being there as they are filled in by groups of pupils and by maintaining an appropriate atmosphere you are obviously more likely to ensure that this is the case. Remember that it is important that the atmosphere minimises the potential for respondents to be influenced by your expectation and peer pressure.

An alternative way of administering the questionnaire is by you reading out the questions to the respondent and noting down their responses. However, researchers trying to do this are the sort that we usually try to dodge in our local high street. The advantage for you as a researcher of using this method is that you will eventually reach the number of respondents required, but it is time consuming and in the process becomes a type of formal interview. Many teacher researchers have found that reading out the questions for pupils to answer on their own response sheets is a good way of administering questionnaires to whole classes. Note that this is especially useful for mixed ability groups of pupils where some respondents may struggle to read the questions themselves.

Example of issues considered in designing a questionnaire

Lesley Curtis, Head of an Early Years centre set in a challenging area of a large city, conducted an investigation into the impact of a training module on the development of Early Years leaders as part of her professional doctorate. The following explains her thinking behind the design and distribution of her questionnaire. Lesley chose the questionnaire as a way of gathering information from a large number of participants. The information/data were gathered through a postal questionnaire. She considered the following in designing the questionnaire before posting out to the participants.

1. The appearance of the questionnaire

She knew this was important if she was to gain a good return rate from participants through the post. The aim was that the questionnaire should look easy to complete, with adequate spacing for answers to the questions. A decision was made to select white paper as opposed to coloured paper. Lesley was aware that coloured paper often had more of an impact when seen (Denscombe, 2003: 97) but white paper was chosen for cost reasons and to avoid any ambiguity through the coloured paper choice. Lesley typed the questionnaire, used Arial size 12/10 font and adequate spacing, and provided a clear introduction to the participants about the research at the beginning of the questionnaire while thanking them at the end for completing the questionnaire.

2. Ethical issues
Lesley was careful to assure participants of anonymity and that they would be referred to as a number on the questionnaire. Their settings would be identified as a school, children's centre, or area role and not by the location or the name of the setting.

3. The design and placement of questions
Lesley's experience of completing questionnaires told her that the questions had to be inviting to the participants. She noted that Robson (2002: 249) highlighted a number of factors in securing a good response rate to a postal questionnaire, pointing out, for instance, that 'initial questions should be easy and interesting. Middle questions cover the more difficult areas. Make the last questions interesting to encourage return of the questionnaire'. Lesley thus chose 16 questions providing a combination of open and closed questions. These questions were placed strategically throughout the questionnaire thereby acknowledging Robson's (2002) point. The university ethics committee examined the questionnaire and made a change to one question. The questions were chosen to elicit information about the participants' understanding of the impact on their practice as a consequence of undertaking an Early Years leadership and management module that Lesley had led. Some questions were set in a list format because they required the participant to rank order the list or tick the list to indicate a preference. Other questions were more open ended, inviting the participants to share their experiences and thoughts about the Early Years leadership and management module.

Analysing questionnaires
If your planning has been done carefully then every question in your questionnaire will be there for a purpose. Your aim will be to elicit data that will help to address the major research questions of your study. With large numbers of completed questionnaires it is a relatively mechanistic task to create a tally of answers for each pre-coded question. From this you will be able to present the overall responses to individual questions. This collation of data is rather more difficult with the more open-ended responses. Here you may decide on a set of categories and place each response in one of these. The answers may then be collated and analysed as with pre-coded questions. There is an issue here of you as a researcher attributing meaning to respondents' answers. An alternative method is to read through the open-ended responses noting each significant point. The end result will be a list of main points mentioned in the responses and the number of times each has been cited.

Once the data have been collated you must then analyse them. This involves describing and explaining what the results show in relation to the respective research questions. Charts and graphs are often used to help express questionnaire results visually while statistical presentation can describe the extent to which certain responses were significant. Statistical analyses using computer programmes such as SPSS are useful for dealing with large-scale samples. Having presented the data and/or analysed them statistically, you will still have to interpret what the data show. Inevitably, any original hypotheses and relevant existing research can be used by you to help make sense of the new findings.

An example of a questionnaire

This questionnaire has been used by tutors for several years to evaluate student opinions of modules on a taught Education Studies course. The data were needed for a number of purposes. Tutors wished to know how the students had found different aspects of each module and their comments were genuinely useful in making improvements for future cohorts. They also needed to consider student responses for each module in order to write an annual subject report that had to be based upon firm evidence. Both the questionnaire results and the annual review were needed as evidence of course evaluation for the external inspection agency.

In this case a questionnaire usefully provided the sort of data required. There were responses on all the key areas that external inspectors examined and the internal annual report required. The information also gave a clear indication of what was enjoyed and found to be of use to students and that which perhaps was not and needed some attention. The questionnaires could be administered in the last taught session of each module and this ensured a high response rate. The students could fill it in reasonably quickly and so it was not seen as an onerous task and came to be viewed as part of the teaching process. Having five pre-coded choices for the first major section of the questions meant that the data could be quickly collated, even by someone who was not the actual lecturer. Currently, completed student responses are typed straight into a database by an administrator but in many universities students will complete such questionnaires directly on line.

If students wished to expand their answers this could be done through the open-ended questions at the end. These open-ended questions were always the most difficult to collate as there could be quite a variation of response. However, they did tend to be negative in nature as 'happy' students were able to respond in the pre-coded questions and usually did not write anything in the open-ended section. Students who had an issue with anything in particular tended to expand on it in this last section. It was important when collating responses to record the comments as a proportion of responses to the questionnaire in general. These questionnaires successfully achieved their purpose of providing student feedback on the modules. It was quick to collect and could be easily analysed. It should be noted that this questionnaire was only one means by which data were gathered on the teaching of these modules. There was also

Excel College
Education Studies
Level Three
Module ED 3001: Investigating Educational Issues (2008/09)

The purpose of this questionnaire is to gain information as part of our quality assurance procedures.

Your name (optional)

Please read each statement carefully and circle the response code which most closely corresponds to your own view.
SA = Strongly Agree, A = Agree, D = Disagree, SD = Strongly Disagree,
NA = Not Applicable / No View

AIMS AND OBJECTIVES

1. The module aims, objectives and forms of assessment were made clear	SA	A	D	SD	NA
2. There was considerable agreement between the announced aims and objectives of the module and what was actually taught	SA	A	D	SD	NA

TEACHING AND LEARNING EXPERIENCES

3. The tutor provided clear and useful sessions	SA	A	D	SD	NA
4. The tutor was accessible	SA	A	D	SD	NA
5. Each session had a clear purpose	SA	A	D	SD	NA
6. The module has stimulated my interest in the area being studied	SA	A	D	SD	NA
7. The module was delivered with enthusiasm	SA	A	D	SD	NA
8. Student contributions to sessions were encouraged and valued	SA	A	D	SD	NA
9. In the module I felt challenged and motivated to learn	SA	A	D	SD	NA

ASSESSMENT/OUTCOMES

10. Assessed work was interesting and stimulating	SA	A	D	SD	NA
11. The criteria for assessment were made clear	SA	A	D	SD	NA
12. Assessed work was returned within a reasonable time	SA	A	D	SD	NA
13. Tutorial support for assignments was useful and productive	SA	A	D	SD	NA
14. Feedback on assignments was helpful and constructive	SA	A	D	SD	NA

SELF-EVALUATION

15. I attended all, or almost all, time-tabled sessions	SA	A	D	SD	NA
16. I feel that I was able to make a satisfactory contribution to group discussions	SA	A	D	SD	NA
17. I found time to do adequate preparation for sessions/assignments	SA	A	D	SD	NA
18. I feel I have engaged with new/challenging ideas	SA	A	D	SD	NA

RESOURCES

19. Reading lists were specific and helpful	SA	A	D	SD	NA
20. Library books and journals were adequate for my needs	SA	A	D	SD	NA
21. Library staff were helpful and supportive	SA	A	D	SD	NA

(Continued)

Figure 7.1   (Continued)

22. Teaching accommodation (space and layout) was appropriate for the needs of the group	SA	A	D	SD	NA
23. Time allocated to the module was adequate	SA	A	D	SD	NA

QUALITATIVE REFLECTION (Please feel free to continue answers to the following questions over the page)

24. What has particularly interested you in the module?

25. How could the module be improved over all?

26. How did you find the methods used?

27. How do you find the style of the tutor?

28. Any other comments?

Figure 7.1   Questionnaire to obtain student responses to a taught module as part of course evaluation

discussion during staff/student committee meetings, informal feedback through individual tutorials, and staff feedback through staff meetings.

Strengths of questionnaires as a means of data collection

1. It is possible to gather large amounts of data relatively quickly.
2. A researcher can compare the responses to particular questions from individuals or between different groups of respondents.
3. The data can be expressed statistically. It is thus possible to make comparisons with other studies (see Blaxter et al., 2006, for more information on questionnaire data analysis).
4. The research may enable overall statements to be made concerning the population, for example, the percentage who left school at 16, the percentage who gained certain qualifications, the numbers who felt that they were bullied at school.

Weaknesses of questionnaires as a means of data collection

1. Questions about complex issues are difficult to compose. Respondents may not find it easy to place their responses into specific categories.
2. The short responses often fail to reflect the varying depth or complexity of people's feelings.
3. It is the researcher who sets the agenda of questionnaires not the respondent. The questions may create attitudes by asking the respondents to comment on topics that they may not have considered previously. Alternatively the questions may not give enough emphasis to those issues which the respondents see as important.

4. A researcher may attempt to overcome such problems by adding open-ended questions. Answers to these will need to be codified by the researcher and to some extent this can lead to the very subjectivity that the questionnaire had been implemented to overcome.

Checklist for writing up the use of questionnaires

When you come to writing up your research having used a questionnaire ensure that you explain:

- why you chose to use a questionnaire in your research;
- who answered the questionnaire (i.e. which type/group of people);
- how many responded;
- how these respondents were chosen;
- any factors that influenced the design of the questionnaire – the type of responses being looked for;
- how the questionnaires were distributed and collected in once completed;
- how well it went and what difficulties (if any) you encountered;
- if there is anything you would change for next time.

Oppenheim (1966) produced a classic text on questionnaire design and analysis, and more recently Aldridge and Levine (2001) also provided useful practical advice.

 Student Activity

Designing a questionnaire

Choose one of the research questions that you wrote at the end of Chapter 4. Design a questionnaire to gather data on this research question. Pilot the research tool with three respondents (these could be members of your research group). Then evaluate the research tool you have designed and amend it as appropriate.

Conclusion

In reviewing the use of questionnaires through the presentation of examples you can see both their utility and their drawbacks. You will have seen how efficient they can be in gathering large quantities of data but we have also cautioned that they have limitations in terms of the depth of data that can be elicited. There is a great deal more that researchers can learn about this heavily used technique through the accumulated experience of their application. We now proceed to look at interviews as another key data collection method within education research.

Recommended Reading

Blumer, M. (2004) *Questionnaires.* London: Sage. These four volumes cover all aspects of questionnaires from design to implementation. The text is very accessible and an extensive range of practical examples and cases is used.

Munn, P. (2004) *Using Questionnaires in Small-Scale Research: A Beginners Guide.* Edinburgh: The Scottish Council for Research in Education. This is a short text on the design and conducting of questionnaires. It is a good practical guide for novice researchers thinking of employing this particular research method.

8

Interviews

This chapter considers the use of interviews as a method of gathering data. We outline how to design and conduct interviews and discuss the issues involved in using and analysing them by reference to a range of examples. We then go on to consider how questionnaires and interviews can be linked within research studies.

The interview constitutes a fundamental research tool in the researcher's kit. Several important decisions need to be made in the planning of interviews concerning the form the interview will take, the role of the interviewer, how the data will be recorded and the final analysis. Interviews may take many different forms. They can vary from being highly structured and very formal to being unstructured and so informal as to appear as little more than conversations between a respondent and interviewer.

Structured interviews

In a more structured interview researchers will follow a set format asking fixed questions. How much they will be able to adapt each interview to varying circumstances will have been decided beforehand but this may be very little. This approach allows for a team of interviewers to interview a large number of respondents and for the results to be standardised. This really is a further development of the questionnaire and is likely to provide quantitative as well as some qualitative data. The advantage this method has over straight questionnaires is that interviewers can clarify issues for respondents and they may also be able to encourage the respondent to expand upon certain answers if this is desirable. A researcher can also note certain non-verbal responses that may help to illuminate answers further.

Unstructured interviews

A less structured approach is likely to be taken when the researcher wishes to place more emphasis on the respondent's own account, perhaps relying on a few fixed questions and prompts. The interview may be very informal and it may become, to all intents and purposes, like a 'normal' conversation. Here the discussion may be very open but the researcher must be careful not to lead the interviewees. These less structured interviews are more favoured by qualitative researchers.

The most 'natural' interactions between researchers and the respondents may take place during participant observation or via a chance meeting whilst a researcher is conducting a case study (Hitchcock and Hughes, 1995 consider interviews in qualitative research in education). A teacher may take the opportunity to sit and chat to a pupil concerning an area she is researching into. The practitioner researcher needs to recognise that these 'chats' are informal interviews and can be a valuable source of data. Teachers actually carry out such informal interviews on a daily basis with a range of people, such as parents, other teachers and classroom assistants, as part of their work. Such data-gathering techniques could easily be used to collect data as part of a practitioner research project.

Selecting respondents

Interviewers must determine carefully who it is they wish to interview. For example, are the views of the head teacher more significant to the research question than those of a Year 7 pupil? Certainly the head will have more power within a school but it depends upon what is being researched. Burgoyne (1994) described what he called a process of 'stakeholder analysis' whereby he interviewed those who were identified as significant people, or postholders, in an organisation in order to gain an understanding of how it operated on a day-to-day basis.

If you are the interviewer you must decide how you will approach the interviewees since teachers, parents and pupils constitute very different interview groups. Teachers are constantly developing their interviewing skills though they will often not realise this. They are used to asking questions in different ways and giving appropriate professional responses to the answers. They will be aware of when it is appropriate, in a school context, to react in a way that shows delight, shock, or annoyance. Thus an interview should be seen as a social interaction and teachers can exploit their skill at such interactions to good effect. Clearly, parents and pupils will also develop questioning and responding skills, though this is done within other contexts so they probably won't share the depth of educational understanding of the teacher and their constructs of schooling and learning may differ considerably.

Sometimes there may be a group of respondents who can be interviewed as a group, e.g. a group of youth workers or pupils participating in particular projects that are being evaluated. Such a group is known as a focus group. Feedback is obtained from the whole group and the results will then become refined through discussion. This can be particularly useful when the research is concerned with future development as suggestions can be made by the project participants through this group discussion. The difficulty for you as a researcher is in knowing whether the group dynamics have affected the results in any significant way. The advantage of using focus groups is that larger numbers of respondents can be involved and are able to feel part of the research project.

Interviewing skills

Research interviews share many of the features of interviews used in other contexts. For example, a training pack on conducting professional development interviews in the teacher appraisal process lists five key considerations:

- the quality and nature of questioning;
- listening skills;
- body language;
- setting and atmosphere;
- overall conduct of the interview.

These key issues are generalisable beyond professional development interviews and are thus applicable to research interviews. They can be elaborated as follows.

Quality and nature of questioning

As an interviewer you need to be clear about what views/experiences you want of the respondent and you must ensure that all key areas are covered in the interview. The 'order' of the questions needs to be carefully thought out by you beforehand. For instance, a respondent will often be initially put at ease with a number of 'routine' or introductory questions. You should ask the questions using appropriate language for the respondent and consider how to present sensitive issues as well. Try to decide whether to keep questions on key areas together or whether it is better to split them up. Be prepared for a range of possible responses by having appropriate follow-up questions ready.

Listening skills

Interviewers must not allow themselves to become distracted and so you should use verbal and facial signals to indicate your interest in the responses. Briefly summarise at various intervals in the interview what the respondent has said to show you are listening and also to check that you have noted the responses correctly. If you are recording the responses you need to skilfully combine this with listening signals so that a relaxed conversational atmosphere is maintained.

Body language

You should consider your own seating position and that of the interviewee and try to adopt an appropriate body position, namely, open rather than closed. Use appropriate eye contact and facial expressions to encourage when suitable and also to offer empathy in response to the interviewee.

Setting and atmosphere

As the interviewer it is usual for you to 'set up' the interview and thus to have control over the setting and, by extension, over the atmosphere that you wish to create. Consideration will need to be given to the timing of interview, the area in which it takes place and whether there will be refreshments. These things are important as they may make a significant difference to how an interviewee will react.

Appropriate conduct of the interview

You will need to treat the interviewee in an appropriate manner in order to elicit relevant information. Clearly, your conduct as a research interviewer should be very different from that of a journalist interviewing a politician or a police sergeant interviewing a suspect! By the end of the session the interviewee should feel good about the interview, comfortable that they have had their say and that someone has listened to them. Close the interview appropriately and discuss any future meetings. It is important you return to interviewees where possible, to show them transcripts, perhaps discuss the interpretation, see if there is anything they wish to add, if anything has changed since, and so on. Follow-up should also eventually extend to sharing your findings with interviewees.

Clearly then it is important for you to hone your interview technique and to be aware of how the quality of the data obtained depends very much on you (see Pole and Lampard, 2002 for a further discussion on conducting interviews). Interviews are an example of social interaction between people taking place in various contexts. Certainly research interviews have a power dimension to them of which interviewers need to be aware. Sometimes this is overt, for example, when a teacher interviews a pupil there is a clear status and power differential. At other times this can be more subtle.

When a newly qualified teacher, for example, has relaxed and informal interviews with her head teacher to explore school staff development issues they will both be aware that they are not equals in this situation and both will act in their own interests. Thus you should realise that a strategic approach in interviews is not just employed by you as the interviewer. It is useful here to consider the seminal work of Becker (1963) and Goffman (1971), who analysed how individuals interpret social interactions in light of their self-image and act as they see appropriate. This 'role taking' also applies to interview situations.

Recording interview data

Interviews take many forms and they are tailored to suit each different research project. One of the most important decisions to be made by you as a researcher is how to record the data. There are several possibilities and both you and the respondent will need to be comfortable with whichever method is used.

Making notes during the interview

You may opt to make notes whilst the respondent is talking. Your difficulty here will be in paying attention to the respondent and engaging in discussion whilst trying to write down the main points. Sometimes the flow of an interview can become disrupted and there may be a pause while you 'catch up'. This may make the whole interview more 'stilted' as the interviewee will begin to concentrate on your ability as the interviewer to take notes. It is also difficult to get actual quotes from respondents as these will take too long to write up. The more structured the interview the less of a problem this is as there will be a clearer list of questions. Even in unstructured interviews you will need to have an idea of what to ask about, so try to draw up an interview schedule, even if this is only a rough outline.

There are many advantages of taking notes during an interview, for example not having to write up the interview later when you come to the analysis stage. You can also read back to the respondent, what has been written during the interview, in order to confirm that the meaning has been accurately recorded and that the main points have been noted.

Recording

Some researchers prefer to record interviews as this allows them to concentrate upon the interviewee and their responses. This is more often the case with unstructured interviews. Some would say that recording makes the interview more relaxed as both the respondent and interviewer are more able to forget its presence once 'in flow'. However, some respondents will not wish to be recorded when discussing certain topics, even if they are promised anonymity. (Whilst one of the authors was interviewing teachers about staff appraisal sometimes the interviewees asked for the recording to be stopped if discussing a particularly sensitive aspect.) As the Watergate affair showed in the United States, recordings can be more incriminating if they fall into the wrong hands, as voices can be identified.

One advantage with recordings is that you can play them back later. However, if your interview lasts an hour then so does the tape and that can involve a great deal of time spent listening. Remember that recordings ultimately have to be transcribed, either in shorthand notes or fully, and this can prove very time consuming. For full-time research teams transcribing such recordings can be a very expensive part of the research.

Remembering and writing up later

For very informal interviews and chance meetings there is often not the opportunity to make detailed notes or record conversations as they happen. Sometimes only the briefest of points can be taken down at the time. The

---

Title of the research: The experiences of managers in a number of education establishments in interpreting and implementing aspects of current government policy.

- The consent of each of the participants was obtained.
- A timetable for the interviews was drawn up on the basis of availability of interviewer and interviewee.
- It was anticipated that each interview would last approximately 45 minutes.
- In-depth interviews were conducted with five managers from different education institutions.
- The interviews took place in the managers' offices. They were recorded with the consent of each interviewee.
- An interview schedule was used. Questions were listed about the education institution, the managers' views about certain significant education policies and how national policy initiatives have been implemented within their establishment. The respondents were allowed to 'talk around' the area in their own way, with questions being asked if a particular issue had not been covered.

Figure 8.1   Interviews with education managers

alternative is to write rough notes down as soon as possible afterwards. If desired you can confirm these with the respondent at a convenient time.

Examples of the use of interviews

1. Individual interviews

The interviews in Figure 8.1 were carried out by an Education Studies student as part of his final year project. As a researcher he was interested in the influence of current policy initiatives on managers in different sectors of education. He had also completed a literature review on recent government policy. It was not possible to use observation to see how these managers interpreted and implemented policy and he felt that questionnaires would have only yielded superficial data. The researcher intended to interview five managers in different education establishments and also to use documentary evidence produced by these institutions. Though the interviews only give an indication of how these particular managers interpreted and implemented policy this was only a small-scale exploratory study and so the researcher felt that this number was appropriate for his purposes.

The interviews were to be in depth and when placed in context provided five individual case studies. The interviewees were: a head teacher of a comprehensive secondary school of 12,000 pupils; a head teacher of a primary school of 150 pupils; the dean of a School of Education; the personnel manager in charge of training at a manufacturing company of 3,000 employees; and the head of student support at an FE college. The researcher was able to gain access to these people in various ways; for instance, he had attended the comprehensive school and so felt able to approach the head, the primary school head teacher was a family friend and the dean was part of his current faculty. Thus it was really an opportunistic sample. The researcher was aware of this and this should not prove an issue providing these facts are made clear when evaluating the research.

Knowing your respondents or using gatekeepers is a useful means of accessing potential interviewees but this can also cause you problems as an interviewer in that the responses may reflect the fact that the people involved may see you as an ex-pupil, student or the child of a family friend. The research here was outlined to the participants beforehand in an email sent by the researcher and a consent form was completed by each interviewee and returned before the interview was arranged. As also agreed beforehand the interviews were recorded. This proved to be a very convenient means of 'capturing' the interview data. The technology for recording is unobtrusive and this made it easier to conduct each interview as a conversation. The interviewer was able to listen and respond without having to worry about notes. Forty-five minutes was allowed for each interview and while some did last longer this time was more or less kept constant.

Having accumulated many hours of interviews, the researcher had to listen to them all, noting the relevant key points. This became the codification of the data. When writing up the account the researcher went back to the recordings to take some actual quotes. The key points and quotes from each interview were shown to the relevant participants for them to verify and add further opinion. In addition, a critical friend of the researcher read some of the notes and listened to extracts of the interviews and judged that the resulting analysis was fair. Once the project was complete the participants were emailed final copies.

Consideration of the practical issues involved in this example may prompt you as a researcher to anticipate similar concerns. If you are looking to conduct similar research you need to consider:

1. How to access suitable interviewees.

2. Obtaining the necessary consent and setting up the interviews.

3. Recording the data.

4. How to analyse the data.

5. Checking the results and feeding back.

2. Informal group interviews or focus groups (courtesy of Jeff Serf, University of Wolverhampton)

In this case the researcher was interested in the views of children on the world around them and to what extent they demonstrated global learning. He was also interested in how they knew what they did, i.e. where they acquired their knowledge. The data were collected through talk during a class session that was recorded. The researcher decided to use the initial stimulus of a television advert for Persil washing powder to promote discussion. The research was carried out in a number of schools after an initial trial in just one.

The researcher was able to obtain qualitative data from the recorded interviews that demonstrated the children's global learning. It was clear that they gained

To what extent do young learners demonstrate characteristic outcomes of global learning in a semi-structured discussion about their aspirations for a 'nicer world'?

Aims   –   to explore young learners' opinions about what actions (and by whom) could/should be taken to improve the world;

          –   to consider the extent to which their opinions reflect the outcomes of global learning;

          –   to identify what/who young learners perceive as the main providers of the 'knowledge', skills and dispositions related to such outcomes.

Target Group – 6–10 members of Year 6 from a variety of schools (four to six in number) demonstrating a range of characteristics i.e. geographical location and socio-economic, cultural-ethnic features.

Method

Method to be piloted with one group of young learners will involve initial stimulus (Persil advert) followed by semi-structured discussion. All phases of discussion to be audio recorded

    Criteria for identifying participants

        –   interested in discussing how to improve our lives, make the world better;

        –   gender, cultural, racial mix.

Each session to last approx. 45 minutes – as free-standing session or as part of PSHE/Circle Time activity.

Phase of Session/ Activity	Key Questions	Links to/Evidence of global learning
1. Initial stimulus – Persil advert – 'Every child has a right to a nicer world' – discussion	Why did they make that advert? Is it true? Is it accurate? How do you know that/Where did you learn about that? What do you think they mean by 'Every child has a right to a nicer world"? Would other people agree with you?	☐ Identifying prejudice, bias and discrimination. ☐ Recognising their own values and what influences them. ☐ Being open-minded and having a questioning approach to the world around them.
2. Your world – discussion	What would make your world 'nicer'? Who would have to do what to make your world 'nicer'? What could you do to make your world 'nicer'? How do you know that/Where did you learn about that?	☐ Recognising their own values and what influences them. ☐ Evaluating the actions of others. ☐ Taking responsibility for their actions and the consequences.
3. Other children's worlds – discussion	What would make the world 'nicer' for others in this school? In England? In the world?	☐ Recognising their own values and what influences them.

Figure 8.2   (Continued)

	Who would have to do what to make the world 'nicer'? What could you do to make the world 'nicer'? How do you know that/Where did you learn about that? Would those children agree with you?	☐ Evaluating the actions of others. ☐ Taking responsibility for their actions and the consequences. ☐ Empathising with others. ☐ Common human experiences, needs and rights to dignity, justice and life
4. Prime Minster for the day – bullet point and feedback	If you were PM for one day, what three things would you do to make it a 'nicer' world? Would everyone agree with you?	☐ ?

Figure 8.2   'A Nicer World': Research Proposal

information from a range of sources and that they did discriminate as to the reliability of the knowledge presented, for example, they recognised the difference between the content of adverts and news programmes. This method of gathering data shows the value of talking to respondents of whatever age. It can be very rewarding, and in this case enjoyable, for both the children and the researcher.

Analysing interviews

There are various ways to analyse interview data and ultimately any researcher must feel satisfied that they have taken the meaning 'fairly' from the interviews. It is important that the series of issues/areas to be analysed have been addressed in each interview, usually stemming from the original research questions. The ease with which the data can be analysed is very much dependent upon how effectively it has been recorded. You will need to look for the patterns that will emerge through the interviews and any particular points of commonality or difference that you will need to mention in the final report. This process of noting key points and linkages is usually termed 'codifying the data' and you will usually do this by reading through the transcripts. Computer programs have been developed that can aid in this process by picking out key words and phrases in transcripts. However try to be aware of any problems that the software may have in deciphering meaning.

The final written analysis may be presented under a series of headings, related to the main research questions, with your overview of what the interviews have revealed. Reporting a series of interviews often involves detailed description and can incorporate variations in the data, giving possible explanations for these. For further guidance on analysing interviews see Blaxter et al. (2006) and also Arksey and Knight (1999).

Example of analysing interviews using codes

Burton and Bartlett (2005) described Steve Tones' investigation into the monitoring and evaluation of the teaching of PE. As part of a Master's degree dissertation Steve was initially looking at how primary school teachers, who had been designated as subject leaders in PE, carried out this role. He became particularly interested in the difficulty these curriculum leaders had in monitoring the teaching of the subject across the school, in particular, how they could judge the quality of teaching in PE when they were so busy teaching their own lessons that they could not see other classes taught. He conducted in-depth interviews with the subject leaders to look into this in more detail. His interview schedule focused on what the subject leaders saw as the strengths of PE in their schools and how these perceived strengths had been identified through monitoring and evaluating the teaching. The system of codes Steve developed to interpret the interview transcripts is shown in Figure 8.3 and an extract from one of the interview transcripts annotated with the codes is also included (See Figure 8.4).

He maintained a good deal of structure in each interview as can be seen from the prompts and the detailed analysis via transcript codes. This was to ensure that the main issues were covered in each interview but also allowed some flexibility of response. Within this approach to analysing interviews we can see that the use of the codes acted as an organising vehicle for the reflections that the researcher made on the interview data. This approach is also helpful when it comes to writing up and commenting upon interview responses.

Strengths of interviews as a means of data collection

1. It is a research method that is adaptable to different situations and respondents.
2. An interviewer can 'pick up' non-verbal clues that would not be discernible from questionnaires, for example, the annoyance or pleasure shown by a respondent over certain topics.
3. A researcher can 'follow hunches' and different unexpected lines of enquiry as they come up during the interview, for example, issues of bullying may become apparent that had not been mentioned or suspected before the start of the study.

Category
Monitoring methods or approaches / M
Sub categories for monitoring methods:
audit / au questionnaire/q
observation /ob structured/st unstructured / us
discussion / di formal time/f informal time / if
reading / re
teaching alongside colleague / tac
assessment of pupils / ap

Category
Evaluation statements or comments / E
Groups:
strengths of PE / st
limitations of PE / li
Sub categories for evaluation statements:
teaching / te
pupil learning / pl
content and structure of PE / cs
extra curricular activities / xa
resources / res

Category
Action planning / AC
Sub category for action plan:
INSET / in
resources / res
assessment of pupils / ap
content and structure of PE / cs

Category
Issues / I
Sub category for issues:
time / ti
resources / res
financial / fi
content and structure of PE / cs

Figure 8.3   The transcript codes

4. A interviewer can collect detailed qualitative data expressed in a respondent's own words.

Weaknesses of interviews as a means of data collection

1. An interviewer may significantly affect the responses by inadvertently influencing or leading a respondent.
2. Interviews can take a great deal of time and may be difficult to set up. This inevitably restricts the number it is possible to carry out.
3. The more unstructured the interviews are then the more variation there is between interviews. The 'uniqueness' of each interview makes collating the data more difficult.

ST	Tell me about the strengths of PE at your school?
VP	We all obviously teach our own class – I like the way we do sports day – **E-St-te**– it's not a competitive thing, it's a personal challenge day – where they are personally challenged rather than racing somebody else – E-St-te you know it is how well they can do – their personal best – I like that I think that is a strength – **E-St-pl** They have a lot of people coming in and helping which is nice from the local College – people coaching for tennis – **E-St-te** we also have visitors – dance and things - which have been quite good. **E-St-te**
ST	Advisory?
VP	People like the Indian Lady – Indian dance – not really advisory – we have had training which is a little different – **E-St-te**
ST	Limitations?
VP	Limitations for the staff or generally the school – well we would like to do more outdoor activities – as younger children – we are sharing space at the moment – with the nursery – I reckon that money is always a problem – because we always want more resources – **E-li-res** We are always losing balls – always start with six balls at the start of the half term – and we never have any at the end
ST	Standards of teaching!
VP	I wish I could tell you to be honest – well I work very closely with my other reception class teacher – and we do very much similar things and she has kind of picked up one or two things that I have done – **M-tac** which worked well– **E-St-te**
ST	How has she picked up on these things?
VP	Well, we plan together – and say what did you do – so we work quite closely together– **M-st**
ST	And have you seen her teach?
VP	I have seen her teach but not watched a whole lesson – I haven't seen any of the teachers teach a whole lesson – **M-ob**
ST	But have seen them teach for some parts of lessons?
VP	Only by looking through the hall – I don't actually watch them– **M-ob-us**
ST	What's your general impression?
VP	Very controlled – quite good – I would say – **E-St-te**

Figure 8.4   Extract from an interview transcript
N.B. VP is the teacher and ST is the researcher

Checklist for writing up the use of interviews

When you come to writing up your research after having collected data via interviews ensure that you explain:

- Why you chose to use interviews in your research.
- Who was interviewed (i.e. which type/group of people).
- How many interviews took place.
- How the interviewees were chosen.
- How consent was gained.
- What the setting for the interviews was.
- The design of the interview and why this was chosen.
- How the data were recorded during the interview.
- How you analysed the data.

- How you fed back the interview data to the participants
- How well the interviews 'went' – mention any particularly good aspects and difficulties you found with the process.
- If there is anything you would change for next time.

Linking questionnaires and interviews in research projects

When considering triangulation, in Chapter 2, it was noted that a mix of methods is often used in order to develop a greater understanding of the issue being investigated. Steve Tones' investigation, referred to earlier, originally used a questionnaire to find out about PE subject leaders' expertise, how they felt about their responsibilies, and how they had set about fulfilling these. The data collected, when analysed, raised certain issues concerning the expertise of these coordinators, the priority of PE within the curriculum, and the time pressures placed upon subject coordinators. However, as we saw, this researcher became interested in one particular facet of his findings and set about conducting in-depth interviews to explore it in more detail. Steve's study provides a very clear illustration of how one method may lead to another as the researcher learns more about his area of interest and the potential and limitations of his chosen method to elicit the quality of data he desires. In Steve's case he realised that interviews would provide more in-depth quality responses, with the questionnaire having provided the initial identification of significant issues. The responses were easy to collate but provided limited data on each respondent's subject leadership role and facilitated only a cursory explanation of the issues facing PE subject leaders.

Many investigations initially use questionnaires, which will then lead on to the development of a series of in-depth interviews. We now present an example which tells us something about the process researchers might use to extrapolate interview questions from questionnaire findings.

2. An investigation into the impact of a training module on the development of Early Years leaders by Lesley Curtis

We saw earlier some of the things that Lesley considered when designing the questionnaire for her research which was undertaken as part of her professional doctorate. Her questionnaire included open-ended questions and she used these responses to identify the themes emerging from her data. These themes were used as a basis for selecting participants for interviewing. Lesley undertook a systematic analysis of the responses, finding that they could be grouped into five main themes: confidence, professional development, effectiveness as a leader, improved or expanded knowledge, skills or experience and reflection. She drew up an interview schedule (see Figure 8.5) based around the themes, noting in the left-hand column the participants who had responded on that theme and summarising the sorts of things they had said.

	Questionnaire	Aspiring Leader interview	Leader interview
Confidence	Participants made reference to confidence within questions 5, 10, 11 and further comments section. In question 5 participants indicated that they decided to enrol on the module: 'To gain confidence' – re participants 11 and 30. In question 10 participants answered that the impact of attending the module made them 'feel more confident' re participants 1, 2, 4, 9 18, 21, 22, 26, 29, 30, 36, 37, 38. In question 11 participants answered that the impact of the module on their vision for five years time was 'confidence' in applying for future Early Years leadership posts re participants 9, 22, 28, 33, 39 and 40. Further comments section highlighted that the module 'gave confidence' to the participants in their roles re participants 7, 20 and 21.		
Professional Development	Professional development was recognised by participants 1, 14, 24 and 37 as a reason for enrolling on the Early Years leadership module. Participants 16, 18 and 38 acknowledged professional development through the Early Years leadership module as the impact on their vision for five years time.		
Effectiveness as a leader	Participants 10 and 28 put forward that they had enrolled on the Early Years module to 'improve their effectiveness as a leader'. Participants 5, 11, 28 and 33 'hoped and recognised the importance of being an effective leader'. The impact of attending the Early Years leadership module enabled participant 5 to 'hope it has made me a more effective leader'. The impact of the Early Years module on the participants' vision in five years' time was for participants 1, 15, 23 and 36 to 'become a more effective leader and operate as an effective leader'. In the further comments section, participant 3 stated, 'I feel this module helped me improve my leadership role'.		

Figure 8.5 (Continued)

	Questionnaire	Aspiring Leader Interview	Leader interview
Improve/expand knowledge/skills/experience	Participants 10, 21 and 28 enrolled on the Early Years leadership module to 'expand/ gain skills, knowledge and experience'. The impact back at settings for participants 3, 8, 16, 28 and 42 was 'developed an understanding of skills', 'improved my knowledge on strategic leadership', 'given me more knowledge'. Participant 35 puts forward the impact of the Early Years module on her vision for five years' time: 'It has allowed me to identify the skills I already have and the skills I need to develop'. In the further comments section, participant 23 states that she has 'increased my knowledge and skills' from the course.		
Reflection	The impact on participant 8, 13, 15, 18, 21, 26, 39 and 42 is that they have become 'more reflective', 'think more', 'reflect on practice'. The impact on vision for five years' time for participant 36 is 'It has empowered me to be a reflective and pro-active Early Years practitioner which will obviously improve my own practice and act as a role model to my staff. Hopefully I will be operating as an effective leader in five years' time'. Participant 39 stated that the module 'helped me to develop a much more reflective and analytical approach to leadership, which reinforced the importance of understanding theory and how this links with practice'. Participant 36 stated that she 'thoroughly enjoyed having time to share leadership experiences with other practitioners and reflect on my own leadership role within my setting'.		

Figure 8.5 Interview schedule linking questionnarie themes to interview questions

She then used this schedule to interview a selection of the original questionnaire respondents (aspiring leaders) along with their bosses (leaders). In this way she was able to probe further an initial issues that had emerged from the questionnaire data. She recorded all the interviews utilising a digital voice recorder, utilising the schedule to note anything additional she noticed in terms of the respondents' behaviours, e.g. when they became animated, embarrassed, distracted, and so on, so that when she listened to the recording she would have additional information which would enhance her analysis of the responses. She then used the schedule again during her analysis of the data to insert relevant responses from the aspiring leaders and their bosses (leaders). A section of the completed schedule is shown in Figure 8.6.

Clearly she couldn't interview all her questionnaire respondents so she had to think carefully about who to interview to ensure that her sample was both representative of the questionnaire respondents and of the emergent themes. She undertook a careful selection process to determine who would be part of her interview sample, taking advice from her supervisor because it was tempting to interview only those people who had been particularly positive about the training or had responded specifically on the themes. As researchers, we have to be very careful to avoid these temptations lest we are accused of bias. Lesley's research was all the stronger for adopting a rigorous stratified sampling method.

Lesley's approach to developing interview themes and questions which in turn partially affected the choice of interview sample is a very good example of how qualitative research processes work, particularly when a researcher is actually exploring the impact of her own practice as Lesley was. This example demonstrates the rigour and care that must be taken to ensure an appropriate extrapolation from questionnaire responses to the development of interview themes and the ethical considerations required to make certain the fair and respectful treatment of all participants.

 Student Activity

Designing an interview schedule

Choosing another of your research questions, design an interview schedule to gather data. Conduct a pilot interview (this could be with a member of your research group). Then evaluate the research tool you have designed and amend it as appropriate.

Conclusion

In reviewing the use of interviews through the presentation of examples you can see both their utility and their drawbacks. They are capable of eliciting important data but the quality of the outcomes is dependent upon how well researchers craft and deploy this tool. There is a great deal more that researchers can learn about this fundamental technique both from other research texts and through practising with various forms of interview questions, reporting schedules and analysis techniques. We now proceed to look at observation as a further important research method.

	Questionnaire	Aspiring Leader interview	Leader interview
Effectiveness as a leader	**Participants 10 and 28** put forward that they had enrolled on the Early Years module to 'improve their effectiveness as a leader'. **Participants 5, 11, 28 and 33** 'hoped and recognised the importance of being an effective leader'. The impact of attending the Early Years leadership module enabled **participant 5** to 'hope it has made me a more effective leader'. The impact of the Early Years module on the participants' vision in five years time was for **participants 1, 15, 23 and 36** to 'become a more effective leader and operate as an effective leader'. In the further comments section, **participant 3** stated, 'I feel this module helped me improve my leadership role'.	**P1** 'I think I am more assertive'. 'I understand my role more'. 'I know where I want to go and I know where we want to go as a staff'. **P8** 'I have because I have done so much more, I feel I have' **P9** 'The course itself has taught me a lot about leadership, working as at team, letting people raise their opinions, asking people what do they think'. **P10** 'Doing the leadership and management module we were actually talking about working in teams and working with other adults so that whole dimension. I hadn't really you know just had experience of but hadn't really looked at or thought deeply about, so that gave me the opportunity for that'. **P14** 'I'm more aware and understanding about people's reactions to certain situations'. 'I'm more observant, I've realised as a leader you need to sometimes just sit back, and watch and see before acting on things'. **P16** 'It's just about being more assertive'. **P18, 21, 26 and 33** made references to 'effective being linked to reflective'.	**L1** 'I would say she is very effective, I would point to several Ofsted inspections where the foundation stage has done very well'. **L8** 'I think she's quite effective in her role, from my point of view she is growing into being effective'. **L16** 'I think delegation, communication, being a role model, sort of and when it arises, not letting things fester, being open and honest with people'. **L26** 'Yes there has been a huge change in her since attending the module' **L33** 'She doesn't sit back and say I don't need to do anymore now, she is onto the next thing but quietly. She will come up to and talk to you as well'.
Improve/expand knowledge/skills/experience	**Participants 10, 21 and 28** enrolled on the Early Years leadership module to 'expand/gain skills, knowledge and experience'. The impact back at settings for **participants 3, 8, 16, 28 and 42** was 'developed an understanding of skills', 'improved my knowledge on strategic leadership', 'given me more knowledge'. **Participant 35** puts forward the impact of the Early Years module on her vision for five years 'time: 'It has allowed me to identify the	**P1** 'It gave me some underlying principles and ideas which were backed by some of the reading did, I still look at the readings now. I use them to underpin decisions that I make and they way that I do things'. 'I keep up to date with journals and Times Eds and things like that now to try and keep up with where we are with Early Years issues and build them into what we are doing here'. **P8** 'More knowledgeable because there are so many different places you can get your knowledge,	**L1** 'I knew very little about foundation stage, so I've leaned on her'. 'We've been on training courses together as well and you know conversed. And we've talked as the leader and the manager about where the department going she knows her stuff'. **L8** 'She's always got every single bit of knowledge and skills she could possibly have I think it is again picking out what is relevant for this particular setting'. **L9** 'She has become more

(Continued)

Figure 8.6   (Continued)

	Questionnaire	Aspiring Leader interview	Leader Interview
Improve/expand knowledge/skills/experience	skills I already have and the skills I need to develop'. In the further comments section, **participant 23** states that the module 'increased my knowledge and skills'.	its not just books, journals, 'internet, talking to other people, liaising with other people, I just think you never stop, do you, you never stop learning'. **P10** 'Only when I did my assignment actually I started reading a lot more of the books all of a sudden I could make the links and it was relevant'. **P14** 'I looked into the Truman theory about storming and norming and knowing how to deal with that in situations and getting through it with people as best we can'. **P16** 'It's just through reading things more I suppose, the hand-outs that we were given and the support from the tutors, and as I say giving you the websites, there's lots and lots of stuff to look up and to read about'. **P18** 'It has given me more skills'. 'The knowledge has grown from what I started with from the course and what I have learnt from the course'. **P21** 'An understanding of the difference between leadership and management'. **P26** 'More knowledgeable because just some of the research you had to do to do the thesis made you look more at where you were working'. **P33** 'And more knowledge when in the leadership role, I mean the course was good cos it sort of provides a background into, you know people who've written about leadership roles and the problems you might face and things like that, so that when you actually are doing some sort of project you can think oh actually I read about that or such and such'.	knowledgeable in her subject'. **L10** 'Her knowledge base increased and she was able to share that definitely. And in role then she's able to put those things into practice and she'd come back and she'd share that a team level'. **L14** 'Sort of for her knowledge as a practitioner, you know she's a very solid member of staff on her sort of subject knowledge of the Early Years'. 'She needs to develop her knowledge of different sort of leadership models'. **L16** 'Looking at different ways of trying to involve staff'. **L18** 'Is aware of the wider issues of the school'. **L26** 'The teamwork, the dynamics of any group and how quickly and easily it can change, she has become very familiar with storming, forming and norming. And she uses that an awful lot'. **L33** 'Foundation stage she's really developing that and is keen to develop it'.

Figure 8.6   An example of an interview schedule combining questionnaire and interview responses

Recommended Reading

Alridge, A. and Levine, K. (2001) *Surveying the Social World.* Buckingham: Open University Press. All aspects of social survey research are addressed in this book. There is a detailed discussion of the design and conducting of questionnaires and structured interviews followed by sections on the presentation and analysis of data.

Drever, E. (2003) *Using Semi-Structured Interviews in Small-Scale Research: A Teacher's Guide.* Edinburgh: The Scottish Council for Research in Education. This is a companion text to that on questionnaires in the same series. It is likewise a good practical guide for teachers and other education researchers thinking of employing this particular research method.

Observation

This chapter considers the important part that observation plays in the research process. How to structure observation and gather data from it are discussed in detail. The strengths and weaknesses of the method are outlined and the chapter concludes by linking observation with other methods of data collection.

Observation as a research method

We spend much of our lives observing what is going on around us. We 'weigh up' situations as we observe them and our resulting actions are based upon data gathered from these observations combined with what we have previously observed and interpreted. Thus observation is an important means by which we come to understand our world. For your research purposes, the type of phenomenon to be observed and your perspective will be key factors in determining how you actually organise and carry out the observation.

Observation can take many forms. It may be formal and overt, as in many psychological experiments where a researcher will note the reactions of respondents to certain stimulations. Similarly, OfSTED inspectors at the back of a classroom with their clipboards will be observing a lesson formally and overtly. Observation may also be formal and covert with those being observed unaware of the observer. Here the 'action' may be observed through CCTV cameras or two-way mirrors, or the observer may be hidden in the crowd. The observer may also take part in the proceedings with the subjects of the observation sometimes aware that they are being observed and sometimes not. Thus a researcher may 'help' in a teacher's classroom whilst unobtrusively observing. In one of our earlier case study examples, on the introduction of the integrated curriculum, a teacher was able to observe lessons whilst giving support to pupils in different classrooms (Chapter 6). In another case study in the same chapter in which a day visit was evaluated, the researcher was observing and taking pictures quite openly but was probably not obtrusive and not really affecting the events and activities in which the pupils were involved.

Thus observation can vary in its formality and openness. It may yield certain amounts of quantitative data or it may concentrate on qualitative descriptions. Much will depend upon how the observation is designed by a researcher and this in turn is dependant upon the type of activity being observed. The observer can affect the situation in many ways and awareness of this influences the design. Certainly it would be difficult to put the case that observation by OfSTED inspectors does not affect the performance of teachers or pupils at all. Also the visiting and observing of lessons by head teachers may not just be for gathering data on teaching and learning in the school, but may also be part of the regular processes that emphasise their authority. Thus, as with other research methods, there are power implications in the use of observation and in the way it is conducted. Montgomery (1999) notes how setting up a teaching observation programme within a school can be seen in very different ways by the teachers involved depending upon how the whole process has been set up and who has ownership.

In setting up observations you as the researcher must be sensitive to the situation. It is clearly inappropriate, for instance, to use overt formal observation methods when researching the counselling of pupils by teachers. Neither will it be possible for you to observe some situations without having a drastic effect on the outcome e.g. if you observe a head of department conducting a staff development interview with a newly qualified teacher you are likely to have at least some impact upon how the interview is conducted and the interaction that takes place. A similar impact would occur if you observed a lecturer giving assessment feedback to a student in a personal tutorial. Certainly other methods of data collection could be considered more appropriate in these examples.

What any researcher needs to do when conducting observation is to consider their ethical position. Observing can in some situations be regarded as a form of snooping so you will have to consider who needs to be aware that the observation is taking place and what its purposes are. Certainly, for any adult working in a classroom to find out that they had been observed even indirectly by researchers and that some record had been kept without them having been informed is likely to significantly damage future working relationships with other researchers. Some researchers would suggest that observing pupils is part of the everyday teaching process and therefore pupils do not need to be informed. This may indeed be the case but pupils still have human rights in place which should be taken into account, along with the need to obtain parental consent. Certainly students in further and higher education and those who are training are classed as adults and gaining their consent needs to be seriously considered. Thus whilst observation is a very useful means of gathering data on what is happening in classrooms and other learning situations, as a researcher you will need to be continually sensitive to the ethical issues.

The techniques employed in the collecting of data are very important in this approach. You may be noting events as they occur openly or you may have to remember them and write them up as soon as possible afterwards. The more formal the observation the more detailed your tally chart will be, resulting in a high yield of quantitative data to be analysed. With more informal observations the schedules will become looser in outline until, in a full participant observation, you will be able to make mental notes under broad headings that you can write up later.

Student Activity

Observation in action

Imagine the complexity of the following situations:

- a classroom of 25 children and one or more adults;
- a lecture theatre with 150 students and one lecturer;
- a workshop where a group of NVQ engineering students are working on lathes;
- a nursery with many very young children and adults involved in a range of activities.

Would it be possible to observe and note down everything that happens? What would govern your choice of observation focus?

Clearly, you will need to plan and structure your observation on the basis of what it is you are looking at. The extent to which the observation is tightly structured will invariably depend upon whether you are seeking quantitative tallies of certain behaviours as opposed to looser descriptions of events.

Often researchers will carry out open or unstructured observations in the very early stages of research in order to familiarise themselves with the topic. These initial observations may raise issues they had not previously considered or help to further refine their research questions. Remember, this can often prove valuable in designing more structured observation schedules later on.

Examples of observation schedules

Schedules displaying the most clearly defined structure are presented first in the following examples, moving on to those that are more open.

Classroom layout

The classroom layout that follows will be familiar to any teacher, pupil and parent. Plans such as these will form the basis of initial observation and analysis.

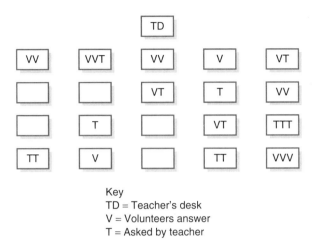

Key
TD = Teacher's desk
V = Volunteers answer
T = Asked by teacher

Figure 9.1   Observation of pupil participation in a traditional classroom layout.

Using these, researchers are able to chart certain patterns of seating arrangements over time and influences such as ability, gender and behaviour. They can also capture data about how a teacher actually controls or influences interactions through seating. Researchers are able to use letters, numbers or some such symbol to show particular activities related to pupils and where they are sitting, such as which pupils volunteer answers to questions, who the teacher asks, or who does not contribute in whole class discussion sessions. It is also possible to chart teacher and pupil movement around the room in relation to such mapping.

In these situations as a researcher you will need to have the ability to identify particular behaviour/actions and to record them quickly. There may be a question of classification here, for instance, in deciding which category a particular action falls. The more categories behaviour is to be recorded into the more detailed the observation becomes, but it is actually more difficult to record as well. Thus whole class observation by necessity tends to be more general in nature. However, here you can focus on one pupil or a small group. It is also difficult to record absolutely everything as it is impossible to write continuously and observe at the same time. In many classroom observations you can overcome this by scanning those individuals or groups being observed at specific intervals. This may be every minute, every three minutes, or every five, and so on. The time slots will depend upon your decision as to appropriateness.

Small group scan

Here a researcher may wish to note numbers or letters for particular activities for each child, e.g. 1 for reading, 2 for writing, 3 for talking to another pupil apparently on task, 4 for talking with another pupil apparently off task, 5 for working with classroom assistant. These numbers can be filled in for each pupil per scan or a brief description may be written in each such as 'playing with marker pen'.

	Peter	Mary	Joanne	Aftar	Dean
1st scan					
2nd scan					
3rd scan					
4th scan					

Figure 9.2 Small group scan

These classroom and small group observation schedules in Figures 9.1 and 9.2 have been derived and modified from original examples given by Hopkins (2008), but variations have been used for some time by other researchers (see, for instance, Wheldall and Merrett, 1985).

As a researcher in this situation may wish to focus on particular individuals within a learning situation. Here the observation may be more detailed as the following examples illustrate.

Individual pupil observations

Figure 9.3 is an example adapted from a detailed study of one child carried out as part of an investigation by a foundation degree student. The aim of such a detailed investigation is to develop an understanding of how children operate on a day to-day basis in an early childhood setting. The student carried out a number of observations using this schedule. These enabled her to develop a picture of the child's daily activities which could be added to data collected from a number of other sources, such as conversations (interviews) with the child, other adults in the nursery and her parents.

The following chart (Figure 9.4) was used by a researcher whilst observing the teacher and two identified pupils over a 60-minute period in a lesson (see the research by Linda Rush in Chapter 9).

Small group observation

A teacher researcher, Angela McGovern, studied the progress of a group of four pupils working with a teaching assistant. This group worked together for 15 minutes every morning for eight weeks. Angela was able to observe the group unobtrusively for a number of sessions and though the classroom assistant was aware that she was observing the children working, the

NAME: Olivia   **AGE:** 2 years 3 months

GENDER: Female

DATE: Thurs. 8 Jan. 2004   **OBSERVATION:**   1

AIM: To observe child over a period of time to see how child interacts with others in a nursery setting.

	9.30 a.m.	9.45 a.m.	10.00 a.m.	10.15 a.m.	10.30 a.m.	10.45 a.m.	11.00 a.m.	11.15 a.m.	11.30 a.m.	11.45 a.m.
Participation in classroom activity										
Child not involved in any activity										
Child watching others in group			✓	✓				✓	✓	
Child in some activity alone		✓			✓	✓	✓			
Child participating in a group	✓									✓
Child following own activity but aware of others										
Talk with others										
Child plays silently			✓				✓	✓	✓	
Child plays and talks to self, not aware of others				✓	✓	✓				
Child talks aware of others, but not requiring responses from them	✓									
Child initiating conversation and seeking responses		✓								✓
Child directing behaviour of others										
Child being directed by others										

(Continued)

Figure 9.3 (Continued)

Child being directed by another												
Talk with adults												
Initiates conversation with the teacher	✓											
Responds when approached by the teacher							✓	✓				
Maintains a dialogue with difficulty												
Contributes when with a teacher in a group												
General attitude	Olivia seemed happy and content playing on her own or whilst with others, joining in when asked and when she wanted to contribute.											
Summary of observed behaviour	Olivia seemed comfortable playing her own game, at times on her own, and also joined in with others with ease.											

Figure 9.3 Observation of one child's interaction in a nursery setting

pupils were so used to having both adults in the vicinity that they didn't notice her observing. Angela used what she termed 'semi-structured observation' in her research (Figure 9.5). The observation schedule consisted of a series of four questions, under which she was able to write notes concerning individual pupils and the group as a whole during and immediately after the observation.

An open observation schedule could alter the focus of the research from the pupils to the role of the teaching assistant in the small group sessions. As a researcher you could look at the type of support given, what was actually taught about writing, and the reaction of the six children during the activity. You could take notes describing the conversations, questions and answers between the children and the teaching assistant.

These observation schedules are the means by which researchers are able to order and collect data appropriate to the focus of study. As with all other methods, observation provides the evidence that enables us to analyse and make judgements about what is happening in different situations. However, you must remember not to allow the data to be reified as the only 'truth' about what is happening. You will have to make judgements throughout such a process concerning when to observe and when not to, what to observe and record and what not to, which actions fall

School *******   **Subject/Topic   English**
Teacher *******   **Date/Time   17.3.03   9.15 a.m.**
Class   Y6

Teacher	0	Pupil 1 Alistair	0	Pupil 2 Richard
Listening to Rosie reading homework.		Finishing off.		Listening to Rosie – watching Alistair.
Praising Rosie – asking Ainsley to discuss Rosie's writing.		Discussing Rosie's writing and listening to next person.		Listening to next person.
Discussing words used in girls' writing.		Listening and joining in discussion.		Listening and joining in discussion.
So many different ways of saying 'said'.		Listening to teacher and class and individuals reading.		Hands up to indicate that he read his writing out to someone at home.
Writing notes re: child's reading of their writing.	10	Listening to teacher praising child and importance of indirect speech.	10	Listening.
Discussing with children how useful it is to pick up from others.		Listening – receiving book.		Listening and receiving book.
What page are we on? Rebecca briefly, Hayley, tell us where we are up to.		Hands up to offer his summary so far.		Looking at text – listening to teacher.
Reading of chapter – do you want to carry on Richard?		Following text.		Following text – reading of text.
Thank you Richard what's Mum doing, how did the author describe the … ?		Listening to discussion.		Reading of text – listening to discussion.
What would be the opposite of chickening out?	20	o.t./listening.	20	Listening to other children's ideas.

(Continued)

Figure 9.4   (Continued)

Lets find out what happens – reading of text.		Following text.		Following text.
Anyone like to make some sort of prediction here?		Listening to other children's ideas.		Listening to other children's ideas.
Listening.		Reading of text 'it seemed – where's that?'		Listening.
OK thanks Alistair well done. Reading of text.		Listening to teacher reading.		Listening to teacher reading.
Reading text. What's he doing?	30	Listening/following text.	30	Listening /following text.
Reading text.		Listening/following text.		Listening/ following text.
Reading text.		Listening/following text.		Listening/ following text.
Reading text.		Listening/following text.		Listening/ following text.
Reading text – questioning.		Listening/following text.		Listening/ following text.
Phew! Why is Helly cheered up now by Kitty's story?	40	Listening/following text.	40	Because she had the same problem with Toadstools.
With partner/gps think of 10 major incidents that happened in book.		Listening to instructions.		Listening to instructions.
Chatting with individuals. Do it chronologically. What does that mean?		Sat by Richard. Discussing with one another.		Sat by Alistair. Discussing with one another.
Talking to me.		Discussing. Writing/ looking through book.		Discussing/ writing/ looking through book.

Figure 9.4   (Continued)

Observing – standing back.		"	"	"			"	"	"
Prompting children – you might come up with more than 10 priorities.	50	"	"	"	50	"	"	"	
With a pair/table groups.		"	"	"			"	"	"
Rotating round tables ????		"	"	"			"	"	"
A lot of you should have same ones – but there is a gp with an important one.		"	"	"			"	"	"
With Alistair and Richard.		"		"			"	"	
Asking children to collect resources/books in.	60	Finishing – handing in work.			60	Finishing – handing in work.			

Figure 9.4   Full lesson script with more able pupils

into the different categories, and so on. As a researcher you will have to interpret what you see in the recording process even as it is happening as well as during the data analysis stage later.

Observing children's use of play equipment

It may be useful to observe set spaces or areas when investigating some aspects of behaviour or activity. For example, Julie, as part of an assignment on child development, wanted to conduct a small-scale piece of research on how young children used playground equipment. She had already helped in a primary school for one day per week gaining experience of working with children. This meant that she was known in that school by pupils, teachers and teaching assistants.

The playground had a climbing frame, a plastic boat, and several different diameter pipes. These were all fixed into a rubberised play safe surface. After gaining permission to observe the pupils at play she had to design an observation schedule. After some consideration she decided to use two different schedules.

How do the children participate (e.g. eagerly, voluntarily, need to be questioned)?

Is there evidence of the children using reading strategies?

Are the activities suitable/suitably paced for the needs of the children?

Do the children concentrate for the entire session?

Figure 9.5   Observation schedule of interaction of pupils with teaching assistant

Schedule 1

This involved observing a different piece of equipment during morning play-time each day. She noted all the activity on that piece of equipment as a sequence of events. This gave her an account of what took place on each piece of equipment for a set period of time. She could then analyse the data for how many children played on each, what activity took place, and how long individual pupils played.

Schedule 2

Julie then observed pupils individually over the morning break time and noted the sequence of their play activities. She was able to observe three children in this way.

Julie now had evidence that she could use in her written assignment on children's play to support her analysis based upon academic literature and sources. The staff of the primary school also found Julie's research helpful because it helped them evaluate which equipment was effective in enhancing children's development through play and also assisted them in understanding a little more about the particular play behaviours of the three children Julie had observed.

Analysing observations

Observations are usually designed to gather data on a number of specific issues. In analysing findings you will need to examine them on each of these issues in turn. For instance, you may have designed a schedule for observing a group of pupils working in a lesson. The schedule will perhaps show over a number of scans what each pupil was doing in terms of a number of behaviours, such as working silently, talking to other pupils, walking around the classroom. You can summarise the data for each of the pupils observed and from this construct an overall account of the behaviour of the whole group in the lesson. If you repeat this on a number of occasions your analysis will show the behaviours over time of individuals and the group as a whole. Ease of analysis in observations is very much dependent upon how they have been recorded in terms of focus and detail.

Student Activity

Designing an observation schedule

1. Arrange to observe a small group. This is usefully done with peers who may also wish to practise conducting an observation. It is best to choose a time when you can all take turns at observing each other for several minutes, such as during an active learning session (with the tutor's agreement of course).
2. Design a schedule containing specific points that you wish to observe.
3. Observe the group for a set period of time, perhaps five minutes.
4. In a few sentences say what the observation has shown.
5. Present stages 1 to 4 to the group for discussion.

Linking observation to other methods of data collection

As with questionnaires and interviews, observation is often used in combination with a range of other methods of data collection. The following is one example that uses a combination of interviews alongside observations.

Title:

An exploration of the strategies teachers and teaching assistants can employ to intervene in children's play and the effect that these strategies have on the learning that takes place.
   Initial research questions:

How do adults and children feel about play?
How do adults and children feel about intervention in play?
How do children play when they play alone/before adult intervention?
How do teachers and classroom assistants currently intervene in pupils' play?
What different forms of adult intervention could be used?
How does play change with different forms of adult intervention?

Methods:

Observation of children's play before adult intervention.
Observation of adult intervention in play and its effects upon the play.
Informal interviews/discussion with staff and children about play.

Findings:

'Distance' intervention, or intervention led by the child appeared to be the most effective for learning. When adults led play from the start and had their own clear ideas of outcomes the play was often less inventive and inspiring.
(*Based on an initial research project carried out by Carole Brown*)

This researcher was aware that children were now starting school at a far earlier age than in previous years. She wanted to examine play as a vehicle for children's learning and specifically the effects of adult intervention in supporting learning through play. She also wanted to observe the effects of three different strategies for intervention.

1. 'Distance' intervention, whereby children are given information or ideas for play away from the setting itself, e.g. through story sacks.
2. The adult is present but intervention is at the child's request.
3. The adult takes an active role in the play from the outset.

The researcher spent several 'practice' sessions observing the children at play to get used to the technique of observation, and also to focus afresh on how children were playing in the classroom situation rather than relying on her pre-formed opinions based upon previous experience.

In the actual research project, several 20-minute observation sessions of each strategy were carried out on two identified groups of children, although other children did sometimes enter the play. Since motives for certain play behaviour could only be inferred from the observations, informal interviews/discussion were held with staff and the children to gain some insight into their feelings about play, adult intervention in play, time spent playing, and so on. The reception class teacher and the two teaching assistants thus also became actively involved in the research.

The researcher was aware that her findings were tentative due to the very small-scale nature of her research and the limited amount of data collected initially. This was the researcher's first piece of research since leaving college many years previously. She did say that carrying out the observations had taught her a great deal that she had not realised about children and how they play. Some of the actions that emerged from the research were for the staff to continue to work closely together, to observe pupils carefully, to discuss their practice, and to share ideas as part of their continuing professional development. Thus the overt use of observation in this case led to a greater awareness among a group of teachers and teaching assistants about the differential impact of these pedagogic strategies.

Strengths of observation in data collection

1. It is possible to see how people behave in 'natural' situations, for example watching pupils play.
2. Researchers can see whether the subjects in the observation act as they say they do.
3. An observer can gather large amounts of data in a short time, for instance several lessons can be observed in one day.
4. Observations may bring certain practices and behaviours to the attention of the researchers of which they had not been previously aware.

Weaknesses of observation

1. Gaining access to situations that would be useful to observe can prove difficult, for example, bullying usually takes place secretively and away from adult eyes and outside observers are not normally allowed to be privy to sensitive or confidential discussions.
2. It is difficult to observe and record at the same time, for example some observation schedules will require recordings to be taken every few seconds.
3. Sometimes it is difficult to categorise behaviour into the pre-determined codes on the schedules, e.g. deciding if pupils talking is on-task or off-task behaviour.
4. The observer may affect the situation, as is frequently the case when a school inspector is viewing a lesson.
5. There are ethical issues of observing people if they do not know that they are being observed. It is also difficult for an observer not to intervene if they feel it is warranted by events.

Checklist for writing up the use of observations

When you come to writing up your research after having collected data via observation ensure that you explain:

- Why you chose to use observation in your research.
- What you were observing.
- The context of the observation, how many times it took place, and for how long.
- Who gave consent and how was this obtained.
- What part you played in the observation.
- What observation schedule was used.
- How the data were recorded.
- How the observations 'went' – mention any advantages you found in using observation as a method as well as any problems you encountered.
- Anything you would change for next time.

Conclusion

Observation is a very efficient method of conducting research and can lead to greater understanding. It is important, however, to always keep in mind the human processes by which the data are gathered when evaluating and making use of the findings. It is not always possible to understand actions by observation alone, for example, why a teacher is treating children in a classroom differently or why pupils are behaving in a certain way. A follow-up interview may be needed. This may turn what is initially perceived as a weakness in the method into a strength, by providing a fuller analysis which will ultimately improve the depth of a whole research project. In the next chapter we look at the use of existing documents as a means of investigation.

Recommended Reading

Powell, G., Chambers, M. and Baxter, G. (2002) *Pathways to Classroom Observation: A Guide for Team Leaders.* Bristol: TLO. The authors consider the use of observation as part of a team approach to school improvement. Through a number of cases they illustrate how observation can be used in creating strategies for change. The text is laid out clearly in the format of a training manual. This book will be of particular value to those involved in school development.

Simpson, M. and Tuson, J. (2003) *Using Observations in Small-Scale Research: A Beginner's Guide* (revised edition). Edinburgh: The Scottish Council for Research in Education. This is a useful introductory text on observation as a research method. It presents practical examples showing how to organise observation, record data and analyse the findings.

10

Research biographies and logs

> This chapter looks at biographical accounts that can supply data for the research or form part of the analysis. Research diaries and logs are also examined as a means of collecting data that monitor a process over time.

What is biography?

A biography is a written account of a person's life or a certain aspect of it. The account may be written by the subject themselves or a biographer who, when the biography is for a research project, is likely to be a researcher. Roberts (2002) suggests that biographical research subsumes various related approaches to the study of individuals. Writing a biography is a useful way of bringing different types of data together into a coherent account in order to explain something about a person. For instance, Swennen et al. (2008) used biographical research to explore the development of the professional identity of two teacher educators in the context of Dutch teacher education. The writing of the biography itself is actually part of the analysis. As this extract from Usher (1995: 1) discussing *auto*biography as a research method explains,

> Autobiography (or telling the story of the self) has achieved considerable prominence in pedagogy and educational research. It appears ideally suited to revealing experience-based learning and in tracking the development of the self as learner ... The autobiographical subject makes himself ... an object of examination ... Autobiography then becomes a process of writing the self, of telling the story of the self through a written text and of writing the text through a culturally encoded meta-story ... This central assumption that a life 'as it really is' can be captured and represented in a text has been increasingly questioned. It is now becoming accepted that an autobiography is not immediately referential of a life but is instead a work of artifice or fabrication that involves reconstructing the self through writing the self. Changing and shifting identity is 'fixed' and anchored by the act of writing. In the poststructuralist story the

emphasis is on writing, the production of text. Life itself is conceived as a social text, a fictional narrative production.

To some extent the way in which an autobiographical account is a fictional reconstruction rather than a life itself also applies to biographical accounts written of others by researchers. The researcher will reconstruct what has been observed or learned about the participant by selecting particular elements, emphasising certain actions, inferring meaning or motive and, as such, by analysing the data as they unfold.

Heikkinen et al. (2007) note that action research reports are often narratives that are expressed biographically because they are located in the context of the evolving experiences of those involved. They propose some principles for assessing the quality of narrative research reports and argue that conceptual tools that are different from the traditional concepts of validity and reliability, which have positivist connotations, are needed to grasp the problem of quality of narratives. According to these principles a good action research narrative:

- acknowledges the past course of events that have shaped the present practices (the principle of historical continuity);
- is reflexive (the principle of reflexivity);
- elaborates the story dialectically (the principle of dialectics);
- produces some useable practices that, in one way or another, can be regarded as useful (the principle of workability);
- involves a balance between Aristotle's notions of 'logos', 'ethos' and 'pathos' with an emphasis on 'ethos' and 'pathos' (the principle of evocativeness).

Examples of biographical research

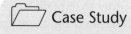 Case Study

The life history of a retired teacher

A student was researching the history of a local primary school that had been built in Victorian times as an elementary school. He had accessed archived county records of the school going back to the mid-1800s. These contained details about the number of children who had attended the school, their ages, and where they lived. There were also records of the school accounts and the numbers of teachers employed. He had obtained pictures of the school from different periods and also newspaper reports of various events and celebrations that had taken place over the years. All this information could be linked to local social and economic history. By also using several other accounts of the social history of the local area the student was able to put together a picture of life over the period of the school's history and its relationship to changes in the community, such as the development of the mining industry alongside farming, the impact of the First World War and also the Second World War, the decline in traditional rural industries, and the development of employees who commuted to nearby commercial centres.

The researcher was able to interview several staff from the school but was also put in touch, via the head, with a teacher who had worked at the school for thirty years and had retired several years previously. This retired teacher was very happy to talk to the researcher about her life working in this school and another one in the area for a short time before that. The researcher explained the nature of the research to the retired teacher and they arranged to meet once a week for three weeks at a local community centre attached to the school. Here they were able to chat about the teacher's life experiences at both schools.

The researcher showed the teacher the pictures and newspaper reports as a stimulus to her memory. He had also prepared a number of open-ended questions about particular times in her career at the school, concerning what she had taught, how things in the wider world had affected her pupils, the health and wealth of the children and local people, and so on. All this was designed to help the conversation flow. The sessions were taped, with the consent of the retired teacher, and the researcher then transcribed these and put them together in the form of a biographical account that he gave to the teacher to correct and approve.

This rich account of the teacher's life at the school was able to bring the other extant documentary data to life. The retired teacher was very pleased to have this account of her experiences and a copy was presented to the school along with the finished research project as an account of the school's history.

To illustrate the use of biography as a means of synthesising and presenting data that have been collected using several research methods we have extracted from a larger study than many of those previously used in this book. This researcher, who worked in teacher education, had had a long-standing interest in the teaching of the more able pupil from when she used to work in primary school as a class teacher. This had ultimately led to her carrying out PhD research into the teaching of more able children in Key Stage 2.

Teaching more able children at Key Stage 2

Title:

An exploration into how effective upper Key Stage 2 teachers manage to intervene with more able children in the classroom setting.

This study explored how eight teachers, who had been identified from various sources as being effective, intervened in the teaching of more able children in their classes.

(Continued)

(Continued)

Methodology:

Classroom observation was the main form of data collection and there was a combination of techniques used:

- audio recordings of teacher talk which were transcribed for analysis;
- field notes using:
  - lesson scripts: systematic observation and recording every two minutes of the teacher and two able children;
  - lesson protocols: non-systematic observation and recording of what the teacher and the more able children were doing and saying during a classroom episode.

Further data were collected from:

- video recordings of selected lessons to provide contextual information;
- the product of children's work;
- digital photographs of classroom activity, organisation and management;
- documentation analysis (LEA policy on more able children, school policies and teacher planning notes);
- informal interviews/discussions with the teacher;
- semi-structured interviews with the head teachers and teachers.

The practitioner researcher outlined three stages of analysis

- Stage 1. Focusing on what teachers do (classroom observation). This involved building up a broad description of how the teachers involved themselves with the learning of the more able children.
- Stage 2. Focusing on what head teachers and teachers say (interviews). This involved drawing on what the head teachers said about the identified teacher: their teaching experience, current position and responsibilities. Whole school issues regarding the identification of and provision for the more able within their schools were also highlighted. Attention was paid, in the semi-structured teacher interview, to the teacher's philosophy on teaching and learning generally and specifically with the more able, and to their conception of ability.
- Stage 3. The telling of each teacher's story. From all of the data gathered a series of 'stories' were constructed, describing in detail the way in which the teacher supports the learning.

(By Linda Rush)

In order to give a flavour of the biographies used in this study, an example of one 'teacher story' is included below. However, for the purposes of this book it has been selected from and adapted rather than reproduced in full. We comment upon the researcher's construction of the story in order to help you understand the things you should be alert to when constructing your own 'stories'.

Teacher story C: Sam

Teaching experience, current position and responsibilities

At the time of this study, Sam had been teaching for eight years but was relatively new to his present school which he had joined as a teaching deputy two and a half terms previously. Prior to this Sam had worked in two schools, one of which had been open plan. Very recently Sam had supported his head teacher and school staff through an OfSTED inspection. In the OfSTED report Sam's 'good support of the head teacher' and his 'ability to combine full teaching and managerial roles successfully' was highlighted. The quality of Sam's teaching was also referred to:

> The majority of the very good [and excellent] lessons occur in the top years of Key Stage 2. These lessons have good pace, questioning is precise and the teacher makes sure that the main teaching points of the lesson are effectively achieved and understood. Praise and encouragement are used well to keep pupils motivated and interested. Classroom management is of a high standard and the relationship between teacher and pupils is good. (Ofsted Report, 1997/98)

Sam's head teacher described him as being:

> ... a naturally good teacher. He has this charisma in dealing with children. They are interested in him and the things that he has to teach them. He works extremely hard. He organises himself well. He's very busy but always has time for anything extra that's needed. He sets very high standards ... He's a sociable person ... His particular strengths, as he sees them, are probably science, design and technology and Physical Education. But he's also a very good maths and English teacher. His one weakness, which he would admit, is music. I don't think he's particularly [strong in] creative subjects such as art. But at the same time he's well organised to teach the creative side and manages to do so, simply because of hard work rather than natural talent ...

However, whilst the OfSTED report had been positive about Sam's teaching and the quality of learning he promoted, it also reported concerns about the school's overall effectiveness. Whole school planning was in its early stages and very little of the perceived school philosophy on the support of learning (classroom organisation and management, assessment, behaviour management) was formally documented. Consequently practice was inconsistent and a lack of continuity and progression prevailed in terms of the children's learning.

Here the researcher has begun her teacher's story effectively by providing a useful biopic of Sam, the context in which he works, the current teaching and learning issues facing the school and two assessments of Sam's teaching skills. In this way we are cued in to consider what the researcher has observed and learned about Sam's teaching approach and in particular his methods of working with more able pupils.

Level(s) of teacher interaction

Out of 174 minutes teaching observed (maths, history and English) Sam spent approximately 45 per cent (80 minutes) of his time interacting with his children at whole class level and 48 per cent (84 minutes) with groups (usually pairs) of children, less so individuals. Evidence of non-interactive teaching was limited – approximately 7 per cent (ten minutes). A negligible amount of time was spent by Sam on housekeeping issues to do with the management of resources, groupings and activities, or maintaining children on task. Actual time spent with his more able at group and/or individual level amounted to approximately 10 per cent (18 minutes).

The researcher makes no reference here to time spent by Sam on behavioural matters – she clearly made a decision, based on her view of what was important, not to explore this issue. She will have legitimated this decision when describing and explaining her research questions. It is important, however, that readers of her research note this as, in a different context, another researcher may have considered that teacher time spent responding to behavioural issues should be a more prominent factor.

Nature of interaction

Whilst Sam initiated the focus of learning and designed the tasks to facilitate that learning, there was much that he did to promote equability of status between him as teacher and the children as learners. For example, in all the lessons observed a warm and friendly climate for learning prevailed in which children's efforts were regularly praised and their contributions valued. Sam had a particularly good sense of humour and his use of language was inclusive:

> ... you are coming up with far too many that I didn't want you to but I will put them down anyway ... (6–8 minutes)
> ... I have put 'show your working out'. This is so important because some of you have got some good ideas about what you want to do ... (12–14 minutes)
> ... it's quite an interesting thing that you are doing ... there is nothing wrong in doing that, like I said, as long as you explain what you are doing ... (32–34 minutes)
> (*Transcript of maths lesson*)

> ... you will recall ... we were looking ... I think we have done pretty well there actually (0–2 minutes)
> ... we want to focus in on what life must have been like for those sailors ... How could we do that? How could I find out ... ? Hayley, what do you think? ... That's an interesting point ... (2–4 minutes)
> ... what were you going to say Alison? ... We are going down a different place here but it is quite interesting ... (4–6 minutes)
> (*Transcript of history lesson*)

Data recorded on Lesson Scripts indicate that the children were listening as respondents rather than passively: 'hands up to answer or voluntary interjection'. There was also plenty of discussion observed between peers – sharing and confirming thoughts before addressing the teacher at a whole class level. At the start of each lesson Sam spent time questioning the children carefully, encouraging them to explain their thought processes and explain their arguments. Questioning at this stage was not used to teach new knowledge, but to help pupils to know and use what they already have (Nisbet, 1990, cited in Freeman, 1998: 23–24).

The researcher is analysing Sam's teaching style by selecting from the lesson transcripts to enhance certain features. She is also relating her analysis to previous research literature. These are elements of good practice in writing up a study but again the researcher must be alert to the power she is able to exert over what she chooses to include/exclude and which literature she chooses to cite.

There follow in the study several detailed examples of teacher talk and pupil talk in a number of observed lessons. Illustrations of board work, and photographs of pupils talking with the teacher as part of the work, are also included to aid the ' teacher story'. We now move towards the end of the account.

Planning of interaction
Apart from the English lesson there was no evidence of short-term planning. However, Sam's medium-term planning was reasonably detailed, identifying learning outcomes, activities, organisation, assessment priorities, resources and notes for further planning. Specific reference to interaction was not evident, but implied through the learning outcomes and assessment opportunities highlighted. This implied interaction was certainly borne out in the lessons observed.

It is worth considering whether a different research method would have revealed this 'implied interaction'. Is the researcher over-interpreting from her evidence by attributing to Sam the indirect planning of interaction? Or does the mix of research tools – observation, access to teacher planning notes, teacher interviews – render the researcher able to reach such conclusions legitimately?

Provision for the more able
Whilst interaction with the more able was limited at group and individual level, the more able did interact with Sam directly during whole class interactions and these were often initiated by the more able and not by Sam. Apart from maths, science and English where the children were (broadly speaking) ability grouped, Sam preferred to group his children socially across the curriculum.

Even within the core subjects overt labeling of groups was not strong. With this emphasis on the social mix rather than the intellectual Sam usually changed the layout of the room on a termly basis so that relationships between children could be shared over the course of an academic year. He preferred to differentiate by outcome and support rather than by task. How well this was done was reliant on his very good knowledge of the children, and excellent expertise of the subject being taught.

Observed practice fitted with Sam's notion of effective teaching:

> ... it is important that you know your children ... know what level they are
> working at. That's Number One I would think. You have got to have a very good
> knowledge of the subject that you are teaching, whatever that subject may be,
> certainly be several steps ahead of the children. You need to have confidence in
> your knowledge of the subject to be able to teach that properly ... Relationships
> with the children ... if you want the best out of them you have to know how
> to motivate them ... Planning I guess [is very important too], having formu-
> lated a plan for whatever the subject may be, knowing where that is going to
> go, where it is going to take you forward. What the next step will be along the
> road, if you like ... (teacher interview)

Sam went on to say that he thought the overriding purpose of teaching the
more able was to 'get the best out of them, thinking constantly about whether
you are challenging them and whether they are working to their full potential' (teacher interview). In the maths lesson different tasks (covering the
same theme) were constructed to take into account a range of abilities. In the
English and history lesson the same task was given to all children and accom-
panied by a prompt sheet which was usually discussed at whole class level.

*Here, although the researcher steers clear of making direct judgments about the efficacy
of Sam's approach with the more able, we can detect her views from such phrases as
'overt labeling of groups was not strong', 'how well this was done was reliant on his
very good knowledge of the children and excellent expertise of the subject being taught'.
A different researcher may have had a bias towards differentiation by task and consequently would have described Sam's approach to the more able less positively.*

 ### Student Activity

Assessing the quality of biographical research

Track down a biographical account of an issue you are interested in or
that you are currently researching. Journals such as *Reflective Practice* or
Education Action Research are good places to look for these.

Bearing in mind the commentaries we have made on Linda Rush's
teacher story, apply Heikkinen et al.'s (2007) five principles (introduced earlier in this chapter) for assessing the quality of action
research narratives to the account you have chosen. Take each principle systematically and assess to what extent the account meets it.
When you have finished consider how well the account met the
Heikkinen et al.'s principles overall.

Now consider how appropriate you think the principles themselves are
as an instrument of assessment and suggest any refinements to them.

The value of teacher stories

Linda Rush's example of the 'teacher story' previously shows how she put together and used data from several sources – OfSTED reports, interviews with the teachers and their head teachers, photographs showing pupils and teachers working and transcripts of lesson observations – to describe how the teachers mediated in the learning of their pupils and in particular that of the more able. Having constructed the stories of the different teachers this researcher went on to compare their mediation techniques using a model of pedagogy that she had adapted from previous research. In this way she was able to extrapolate from highly specific classroom-based research to a theoretical model found in the literature.

As in other highly participative research forms, it is important that the researcher shares the final story with the teacher whom it portrays and that they discuss it together. This helps to maintain the researcher's accountability to the subjects of the research and is also an essential part in ensuring the validity of the study. It is always important to remember that, whilst providing very interesting, accessible and relatable accounts of how teachers work, teacher stories and biographies such as these have been constructed on the basis of how the writer interprets the evidence.

The use of biographical accounts constructed by the teachers and pupils who make up the research population themselves is also a useful means of generating data. These accounts may be about their whole career, their daily lives or some specific event. Some researchers will ask respondents to write fictional accounts of their work or aspects of their lives based upon real life examples (see Clough and Nutbrown, 2007). This encourages them to reflect upon their experiences without having to disclose particular details. Such narratives can then be used in discussions with the respondents. Other researchers will use this device because they feel it will lead them to a deeper understanding of the issue or data. Waterland, a head teacher researching the experiences of children, parents and staff at the beginning of a school year, chose to recreate the product of the months of observation as a fictional account because 'it is only by constructing the world the child experiences within our own imaginations that we can make the world better' (2001: 138). Chapman explains that such personal narrative as a research device is congruent with a shift away from positivism toward interpretivism, where meaning has become a central focus. She reminds us that

> there is nothing new about storying; the human need to make meaning of life's events, traumas and crises, as well as to (re)arrange the vagaries of everyday chaos into a narrative that structures unpredictability and tames uncertainty is ancient. We tell our lives, daily, in a repetition of stories, beginning and ending, rewriting and reforming ourselves ... Oral cultures, written cultures, machine cultures, electronic cultures – the common thread is the self-story. (1999: 2)

Checklist for writing up the use of biographies

When you come to writing up your research after having collected data via biographies ensure that you explain:

- Why you chose to use biography(ies) in your research.
- Who the participants were and how they were chosen.
- How you obtained consent from the participants.
- How the biographies were written, i.e. any structure or stimuli that were designed and used.
- How you fed back and validated the biographies with the participants.
- How well the process of writing the biographies went – mention any particular strengths you found in using this method of data collection and any problems you encountered.
- Anything you would change for next time.

Research diaries and logs

Another way of creating written accounts that can monitor changes over time, and also record people's feelings and reactions to them, is to keep research diaries. They are different from a biography in that they form an on-going account rather than a description that is put together later. These can be written by teachers, pupils, researchers, or anyone else concerned with a particular research project. Mutually agreed headings can be used that reflect the research focus and can act as prompts for the writer. If these are written at what are agreed as appropriate intervals of perhaps every day, or week, or month, these diaries can provide interesting accounts of developments or even daily life as it happens. There are many examples of the use of diaries, which in shortened form are often referred to as logs, currently being developed in education. For example, pupils fill out progress logs with guidance from form tutors and class teachers, and teachers may have professional development logs that are annually updated.

The research of Clandinin and Connelly (1994) encouraged students to use life stories to reflect on their experiences as learners, teachers, or administrators. The following are logs written by student teachers during their training. They are taken from examples collected by Malcolm Dixon of Liverpool John Moores University and used in discussion with current students. These logs show differing amounts of factual description or reflection by the authors depending upon the particular requirements. As the student teachers progress through their training they are requested to research their own practice using the professional standards for the award of QTS as the criteria for their observations and judgements. Such logs might be presented as part of a trainee teacher's evidence for a school-based research task or to show their

Name:	Date: 15.4.02 – 19.4.02

This week I have discovered how difficult not only differentiation within the classroom is (12 SEN children in the class), but also that spending quality time with each group appears to be impossible! During this week I feel I have not moved passed the low attainers, therefore the average/high attainers have been neglected. This means that the children are being held back, therefore I need to devise a system to ensure **all** children have equal quality time spent with them. Due to this I aim to focus on one group each day.

A positive feature I have noticed that appears to be beneficial to the children is the introduction of a vocabulary/spelling book. At the beginning of each lesson I have asked the children to write two definitions of specialist vocabulary pertaining to the lesson. This way the children can refer to the definitions throughout the lesson, which not only saves time on explanations, but also reinforces the meanings of words. Coupled with this, since the children can bring the book to me for spellings it does not detract my attention from the task I am engaged in with other children from the group. After reflecting upon this week teaching I feel it is important to devise another strategy to assist the children with their interpretation of words. Therefore it is my intention to produce a word bank that can be placed in the middle of the table during lessons. This will need to be differentiated so as the low attainers do not have difficulty with reading the words in the bank.

Another issue that needs attention is differentiating work amongst the low attainers. Louise and James are very low attainers and cannot keep up with the other children on their table. This means additional resources will need to be devised for these two children.

Figure 10.1   Student teacher weekly reflective log

growing professional competence. Teacher training tutors have also used cross-sections of such evidence to exemplify features of the 'training journey' within broader research into teacher education and training. Drever and Cope (1999), for instance, found that elements of theory taught on an ITE course could be detected within student teacher narratives, albeit somewhat subliminally! Many PGCE courses also include a Master's element within them so there is a greater imperative to reflect on practice in relation to theoretical perspectives. Logs and diaries can provide an excellent way of presenting such reflection.

Logs and diaries can provide fascinating research data which, although of a biographical nature, can enlighten educational communities in a broader sense. Although it is not possible to generalise from one person's experience it is legitimate to use this evidence to establish some aspects for further investigation. For instance, a trainee probation officer, an NQT or a new youth worker and their mentors may keep independent weekly logs of their respective experiences in working together. It may emerge from these that there are misconceptions or different conceptions about the role of the mentor in the mentee's development. In addition to these two individuals working through these issues together, it would also be possible for the research to be broadened to other pairs to explore issues of role perception within mentoring.

Name:	Week Ending: 1st Feb 2002

1.   Significant progress made in relation to the standards for QTS

This week I have managed to teach all of the numeracy lessons as well as two science lessons and one Physical Education lesson. I have also taken individual groups from literacy lessons to the computer suite to develop their ICT skills in this subject area. I have also observed and worked with a science specialist on a variety of activities aimed at developing their skills in fair testing and recording results.

2.   Areas in need of further work/development in relation to the standards for QTS

I need to continue completing my pupil progress records as well as making some progress on my school-based activities. I am nearly up to date on my planning but I still need to catch up on some of my lesson evaluations. I also need to start gathering appropriate school documentation to add to my school file, which is now taking shape.

Mentor Comment: The planning is very important, the amount of time you are taking on this proving to be very successful.

3.   Personal view of points for action next week

- Complete planning literacy, science and PE lessons.
- Make more progress recording and reporting on pupils' work.
- Plan for time to complete some school-based activities.
- Catch up on my lesson evaluations.

Mentor Comment: Just try to pace yourself.

4.   Other Points

I now feel that I have really settled into this teaching practice. I have developed some good relationships with the pupils in both of the classes that I teach and I am really enjoying my teaching. I have a good relationship with the teachers and several have given me some good advice and support on my planning and other areas of teaching. I think that I have gained the trust and respect of the children and this has become a big help to my teaching. All aspects are going very well.

Mentor Comment: Fully agree, you look like part of the furniture – very comfortable and at home in the classroom.

Figure 10.2   Student teacher weekly self-monitoring form

 Student Activity

Writing a research log

1.   Identify something that you would like to monitor or chart over a period of time. This may be something in your own life, such as academic studying, travelling, or interacting with different groups of people. It may be something in your environment, such as use of the learning centre at different times or student attendance at different teaching sessions. It could be something in daily school life, such as the frequency and type of homework given to a particular group of pupils or the use of playground equipment by children in their break

times. It may be pupil focused, such as the behaviour of particular pupils or the quality of their written work.

2. At the beginning of a new exercise book list what you consider to be the key factors about the particular focus chosen.

3. In the exercise book write between a paragraph and half a page at regular intervals, such as at a set time every day, or after several days, on what has happened in relation to your chosen focus since the previous entry. Be sure to address the key factors. You may wish to use these key factors as sub-headings. Ensure that each entry is clearly labelled with the date and time.

4. After two weeks summarise the contents of the log. Be sure to address the key factors and to say what significant things have happened over this time.

5. Report on how you designed the log and findings to your research group.

Checklist for writing up the use of diaries and logs

When you come to writing up your research after having collected data via logs ensure that you explain:

- Why you chose to use your log, or logs from other participants, in your research.
- Any criteria or format that was decided on for writing the log.
- How often and when the log entries were completed.
- How useful, or not, the logs were in producing the quality of data you were looking for.
- Any strengths or weaknesses you found with using this method of data collection.
- Anything you would change for next time.

Conclusion

The use of biography or logs and the fictionalising of accumulated individual accounts are useful ways of describing and analysing processes and experiences within education. Increasingly researchers are using this method; see for instance Miller and West (2003), whose work has focused on auto/biographical approaches to research on adult learning and on processes of learning from experience. Or Chapman (1999), who contends that educators engage so routinely in 'the discursive practices that fix educational subjects', such as grading, evaluating and assessing, that they are unnoticed as a form of 'storying'.

Those of us in education know this, of course. Education is but one facet of the bureaucratic machine that writes us all – and in which we write or story ourselves, willingly or not; we fill in those forms, daily, weekly, monthly, yearly, as if our very lives depend upon them, as they do. (1999: 2)

Recommended Reading

Elliott, J. (2005) *Using Narrative in Social Research: Qualitative and Quantitative Approaches.* London: Sage. This book provides an introduction to the use of narrative methods in research. The author discusses the importance of narrative as a means of developing understanding. She outlines methods of collecting and analysing data by these methods. These are well worth considering as a means of researching into different people's experiences of education.

Roberts, B. (2002) *Biographical Research.* Buckingham: Open University Press. A range of data collection approaches that come under the heading of biography are discussed here. Methodologies are outlined that education researchers will find useful but may not have previously considered, such as oral history and narrative analysis.

11

Use of existing documents

This chapter considers the variety of existing (extant) documentary material that provides useful data for education research. This can take many forms, ranging from historical school records and national curriculum documents to OfSTED reports on specific schools and records of pupil attainment within a particular class. We provide examples of and discuss how a range of documents can be used, from pupil reports to schemes of work. The chapter then goes on to consider the analysis of published curriculum materials used by teachers and photographic evidence analysed by pupils.

Existing written evidence

There is already much qualitative and quantitative data written about every school and place of education that can be used by researchers, e.g. OfSTED reports, national curriculum assessment data, external examination results, attendance and pupil exclusion statistics. There is also a great deal of documentation produced at all levels of the education service, e.g. school prospectuses, development plans, and policies on all aspects of the curriculum. There is also other written documentation that may be helpful, if less readily available, such as the minutes of staff, department, and governors' meetings. These sources can therefore provide valuable data about all aspects of life in different educational settings. Indeed Prior (2003) contends that such documents form a field for research in their own right.

As an education researcher you will always need to bear in mind who has been involved in producing documents and collecting this official information, the type of questions people will have been asking and also what they would not have looked at. It is important to remain critical and to recognise the different ways in which information can be officially presented. The deconstruction of such documents and data is an important area of research in itself. For example,

NAME	John Hughes
DATE	Dec 1964
GROUP	1
No. IN GROUP	8
AGE	9.11
AVERAGE AGE	10.5
ENGLISH	Very Good – has a good grasp of the essentials
SPELLING	Very Good
COMPOSITION	Excellent ideas and always an interesting composition
MATHEMATICS	Good, but must try harder with problems
GENERAL KNOWLEDGE	Very good – gives sensible answers
CRAFT	Good on the whole, but often careless
REMARKS	John's handwriting has improved, so his work is more easily understood. He is well able to concentrate, and gains knowledge from his extensive reading. He is very musical, and has a good sense of rhythm.

Figure 11.1 A report of a pupil in a small primary school in rural England in 1964

school performance statistics may, if taken at face value, show changes in pupil achievement over time. However, it is important to question why these statistics were compiled, how they were collected, and what they do or do not tell us about the performance of individual pupils. As Prior counsels, 'content is not the most important feature of a document' (2003: 26). Similar analysis can be undertaken on the construction of written documents, such as official codes of conduct and school prospectuses. Such analysis will give some indication about what is valued, at least officially, in the education system.

Reporting on pupil progress

Consider the following reports to parents of pupil progress. These cover pupils from different generations of the same family and as such they are interesting historical documents in themselves (note all names have been changed). They provide useful material for research into the reporting of pupil achievement, to parents, curriculum development, pupil assessment, the work of teachers, expectations of pupils' achievement, and so on. They also give a fascinating insight into how these things have changed (or not!) over the years and you can draw your own conclusions about the level of care and detail taken over them and what this implies about the ways in which a teacher's work has changed.

| Peter Hughes | Report for the School Year 2002–2003 | Year Five |

Sessions (Half days) this year: <u>310</u>
                                     310

Attendances: 100%   ☑   Unauthorised Absences: ☐
Punctuality: Satisfactory   Improvement needed

S.E.N._____

> Throughout this report progress in learning is shown as:-
> (A)   is working beyond this target
> (B)   has achieved this target
> (C)   working towards this target

There will be an opportunity to discuss your child's report at parents' evening in July.

ENGLISH – SPEAKING AND LISTENING	A	B	C
• Talks and listens with confidence in an increasing range of contexts		✓	
• In discussion listens carefully, making contributions and asking questions that are responsive to others' ideas and views			✓
• Uses appropriately some of the features of standard English vocabulary and grammar		✓	
• In discussion, shows understanding of the main points		✓	

ENGLISH – READING	A	B	C
• In responding to a range of texts, shows understanding of significant ideas, themes, events and characters, beginning to use inference and education		✓	
• Refers to the text when explaining views		✓	
• Locates and uses ideas and information		✓	
• Reads a range of texts fluently and accurately	✓		

ENGLISH – WRITING	A	B	C
• Ideas are often sustained and developed in interesting ways and organised appropriately for the purpose of the reader		✓	
• Is beginning to use grammatically complex sentences, extending meaning		✓	
• Full stops, capital letters and questions marks are used correctly and is using punctuation within the sentence		✓	
• Handwriting style is fluent, joined and legible		✓	
• Writing is often organised, imaginative and clear		✓	
• Spelling is usually accurate, including that of common, polysyllabic words		✓	

(Continued)

Figure 11.2   (Continued)

MATHEMATICS	A	B	C
• Multiply and divide any positive integer up to 10,000 by 10 or 100 and understand the effect			✓
• Order a given set of positive and negative integers		✓	
• Use a decimal notation for tenths and hundredths		✓	
• Round a number with one or two decimal places to the nearest integer			✓
• Relate fractions to division and to their decimal representations			✓
• Calculate mentally a difference such As 8006 – 2993		✓	
• Carry out column addition and subtraction of positive integers less than 10,000		✓	
• Know by heart all multiplication and division of a three-digit by a single-digit integer		✓	
• Carry out long multiplication of a two-digit by a two-digit integer		✓	
• Carry out long multiplication of a two-digit by a two-digit integer			✓
• Understand areas measured in square centimetres (cm2) understand and use the formula in words 'length x breadth' for the area of a rectangle		✓	
• Recognise parallel and perpendicular lines, and properties of rectangles		✓	
• Use all four operations to solve simple word problems involving numbers and quantities including time, explaining methods and reasoning			✓

MATHS – SHAPE SPACE AND MEASURE	A	B	C
• Makes 3-d mathematical models by linking given faces or edges and draws common 2-d shapes in different orientations on grids		✓	
• Reflects simple shapes in a mirror line		✓	
• Chooses and uses appropriate units and instruments, interpreting, with appropriate accuracy, numbers on a range of measuring instruments		✓	
• Finds perimeters of simple shapes and finds areas by counting squares		✓	

MATHS – HANDLING DATA	A	B	C
• Collects discrete data and records them, using a frequency table		✓	
• Understands and uses the mode and range to describe sets of data			✓
• Groups data, where appropriate, in equal class intervals, represents collected data in frequency diagrams and interprets such diagrams		✓	
• Constructs and interprets simple line graphs		✓	

Figure 11.2   (Continued)

SCIENCE – SCIENTIFIC ENQUIRY	A	B	C
• Recognises that scientific ideas are based on evidence		✓	
• In own investigative work, decides on an appropriate approach (for example, using a fair test) to answer a question		✓	
• Where appropriate, describes or shows, in the way the task is performed, how to vary one factor whilst keeping others the same		✓	
• Where appropriate, makes predictions		✓	
• Selects suitable equipment to use and makes a series of observations and measurements that are adequate for the task		✓	
• Records observations, comparisons and measurements, using tables and bar charts		✓	
• Begins to plot points to form simple graphs and uses these graphs to point out and interpret patterns in the data		✓	
• Begins to relate conclusions to these patters and to scientific knowledge and understanding, and to communicate them with appropriate scientific language		✓	

SCIENCE – MATERIALS AND THEIR PROPERTIES	A	B	C
• Describes differences between the properties of different materials and explains how these differences are used to classify substances such as solids, liquids and gases		✓	
• Describes some methods, such as filtration and distillation, that are used to separate simple mixtures		✓	
• Uses scientific terms, such as evaporation or condensation, to describe changes		✓	
• Uses knowledge about some reversible and irreversible changes to make simple predictions about whether other changes are reversible or not		✓	

INFORMATION AND COMMUNICATIONS TECHNOLOGY	A	B	C
• Creates sequences of instructions to control events and understand the need to be precise when framing and sequencing instructions when using logo and turtle		✓	
• Understands how ICT devices with sensors can be used to monitor and measure external events such as using ecotoy and digital thermometers		✓	
• Explores the effects of changing the variables in an ICT		✓	
• Discusses their knowledge and experience of using ICT and their observations of its use outside school	✓		
• Assesses the use of ICT in own work and can reflect critically in order to make improvements in subsequent work	✓		

(Continued)

Figure 11.2   (Continued)

INFORMATION AND COMMUNICATIONS TECHNOLOGY	A	B	C
• Adds to, amends and combines different forms of information from a variety of sources when working with Excel	✓		
• Uses ICT to present information in different forms and shows awareness of the intended audience and the need for quality in their presentations, e.g. when word processing and using digital camera	✓		
• Compares own use of ICT with other methods and with its use outside school		✓	

RELIGIOUS EDUCATION (following LA agreed syllabus)	A	B	C
• Has learnt about the significance of some number in a range or world faiths		✓	
• Has developed understanding of the journey of life and some rites of passage		✓	
• Has begun to explore the significance of water in some world religions		✓	
• Has discussed, with sensitivity, moral issues linked to the use of the world's resources, especially water		✓	
• Developing a greater sensitivity to their own spiritual growth and acknowledging the spirituality of others		✓	

HISTORY	A	B	C
• Uses knowledge and understanding of aspects of the history of Victorian Britain, Ancient Greece and the wider world to describe features of past societies and to identify changes within and across periods		✓	
• Is beginning to select and combine information from different sources and is beginning to produce structured work, making appropriate use of dates and terms		✓	
• Shows how some aspects of the past have been represented and interpreted in different ways		✓	

GEOGRAPHY	A	B	C
• Recognises and describes physical and human processes when studying rivers and water		✓	
• Describes how people can both improve and damage the environment and explains views about environmental change		✓	
• Uses a range of books, maps, pictures and ICT in investigations and communicates findings clearly		✓	
• Is beginning to read, understand and interpret a range of maps in different scales		✓	

Figure 11.2   (Continued)

ART	A	B	C
• Explores ideas and collects visual and other information to help them develop work when using sketch books for work on landscapes		✓	
• Uses knowledge and understanding of materials and processes to communicate ideas and meanings, and makes images and artefacts, combining and organising visual and tactile qualities to suit own intentions		✓	
• Compares and comments on ideas, methods and approaches used in own and others' work, relating these to the context in which the work was made, e.g. Victorian paintings and Ancient Greek pottery		✓	
• Adapts and improves work to realise own intentions		✓	

DESIGN TECHNOLOGY	A	B	C
• Generates ideas by collecting and using information when studying switches and the Ironbridge		✓	
• Takes users' views into account and produces step-by-step plans		✓	
• Communicates alternative ideas using words, labelled sketches and models, showing awareness of constraints		✓	
• Works with a variety of materials and components with some accuracy, paying attention to quality of finish and to function when designing structures		✓	
• Selects and works with a range of tools and equipment		✓	
• Reflects on recipes as they develop bearing in mind the way the bread will be used		✓	
• Identifies what is working well and what could be improved		✓	

MUSIC	A	B	C
• Sings and plays for performance, from ear and simple notation, with awareness of how different parts fit together		✓	
• Through listening to a variety of music explores how sounds and music reflect different moods and intentions		✓	
• Can improvise rhythmic phrases within a group and can suggest improvements to own and others' work		✓	

PHYSICAL EDUCATION	A	B	C
• Links skills, techniques and ideas and applies them accurately and tactically when playing invasion games	✓		
• Performances shows precision, control and fluency, understands composition in dance and gymnastics		✓	

(Continued)

Figure 11.2 (Continued)

PHYSICAL EDUCATION	A	B	C
• Compares and comments on skills, techniques and ideas used in own and others' work, and uses this understanding to improve performance	✓		
• Explains and applies basic safety principles in preparing for exercise	✓		
• Describes what effects exercise has on the body, and how it is valuable to fitness and health	✓		

P.S.H.E.	A	B	C
• Is learning about self as a growing and changing individual with own experiences and ideas, and as a member of the community		✓	
• Is becoming more mature, independent and self-confident		✓	
• Is learning about the wider world and the interdependence of communities within it			
• Is developing a sense of social justice and moral responsibility and is beginning to understand that own choices and behaviour can affect local, national or global issues and political and social institutions		✓	
• Is learning how to take part more fully in school and community activities			✓
• Is learning how to make more confident and informed choices about health and environment, to take more responsibility, individually and as part of a group, for own learning, and to resist bullying			✓

CONSIDERATION FOR OTHERS	PRESENTATION OF WORK Takes a pride in work:
• Always polite and considerate	• always ✓
• Polite and considerate most of the time	• usually
• Sometimes needs to be reminded of the needs of others ✓	• sometimes

COMMENTS

ENGLISH
Peter is a fluent reader. He has a good comprehension of the text and has developed the ability to use less obvious clues to enhance his understanding of characters and plot. He has begun to analyse how words and phrases can be used to make a text more interesting. Peter writes well and is beginning to consider the most appropriate language–style to use for different types of writing. He needs to improve focus and concentration to maintain his quality throughout a longer piece of writing. Peter has very good spelling. He has learned important skills in self-editing for spelling, punctuation, grammar and style of writing and now needs to use these regularly in his own work.

Figure 11.2 (Continued)

MATHEMATICS
Peter has good numeracy skills. His responses to mental arithmetic questions are generally quick and accurate. He is beginning to develop skills in applying his knowledge to simple problems by working out which numeracy method is appropriate to use in which problem. This will need continued revision to ensure the skills learned become fluent. Peter's written work is usually accurate, however he needs to develop the habit of checking his calculations to ensure the minimum of errors. Peter tells me he lacks confidence to write answers unless he is certain they are correct, this may explain the difference between his generally competent performance in whole class discussion and less confident in written work. Let's see Peter 'Go for it!' next year – don't worry about the occasional mistake.

SCIENCE
Peter has enjoyed this year's science, he has a good understanding of the topics covered and he has a developing understanding of scientific enquiry. Peter is able to draw upon past knowledge to make predictions and to question the veracity of results. Now he needs to be more exacting in his analysis of results and to take a more active role in decision making when conducting experiments.

GENERAL COMMENTS
Peter has a great deal of potential. He is sufficiently intelligent to do well academically and he has the charisma of a leader. These are not mutually exclusive.
Peter has made good progress in English and he now needs to put similar effort into his Maths. I hope to see Peter responding positively to the opportunities and responsibilities he will be offered next year.
Class teacher's signature   Date: 21.6.03

HEAD TEACHER'S COMMENT
Excellent attendance; now let us see this matched with behaviour and motivation!! Peter you can do it!
Signature   Date: July 03

Figure 11.2   Report of a pupil from a primary school in a town in the West Midlands in 2003

The contrast between these reports cannot fail to strike us and raises different questions depending on our views of education, reporting and so on. For instance, one parent might ask how the first report could possibly convey any meaningful information about John's progress. Another may ask whether the extensive data made available on John's nephew, Peter, nearly forty years later, are necessary or comprehensible.

We can see that a whole host of research uses might be made of such documents. Written documents, whilst providing evidence themselves,

HIGH SCHOOL FOR BOYS

CONFIDENTIAL REPORT ON: John Hughes   Form: 3W   Date: Summer 1969
Age: 14.6   Average Age: 14.3   Times Absent: 24   Times Late: Invariably

SUBJECT	Term %	Exam %	REMARKS	
ENGLISH	63	42	Produces quite good work.	BW
GEOGRAPHY	17	24	Still very poor.	RP
HISTORY	52	31	Careless. Unsatisfactory. Work rarely legible.	ACB
LATIN	62	31	He could have done well in this subject.	A
FRENCH	62	18	He should have done better.	PJH
MATHEMATICS	44	24	Much more care is needed.	PAD
PHYSICS	63	29	His work has deteriorated badly.	KH
CHEMISTRY	55	18	He could do much better.	NJ
BIOLOGY	35	23	He has made very little effort.	CP
ART	39	57	Has relaxed in effort somewhat though examination work was fairly good.	DHW
MUSIC		61	He has ability but seems afraid to use it.	NB
WOODWORK	37	24	He tries hard but is rather slow.	BEL
RELIGIOUS EDUCATION			Works well.	PR
PHYSICAL EDUCATION			Satisfactory.	LW

GENERAL REMARKS
A bad report. He seems to be cultivating a lackadaisical approach to work

Form Master

Figure 11.3   Report of a pupil in a small town secondary state grammar school in 1969

are also useful in discussion with the significant parties. For instance, it is interesting to discuss reports with teachers who write them, parents who receive them and pupils who are written about. It stimulates thoughts on many personal aspects and memories of school life. In this way such documents may help to produce rich biographical accounts. Consider John's secondary school report of several years later. Certainly there is a 'story' to be told of his educational journey through primary school into secondary, and eventually, if the evidence were gathered, into employment.

In looking back at his father's report from the same school over thirty years previously, what is most striking is how little change had been made in the reporting format and comments of the two reports. The names of the curriculum subjects are in some cases significantly different, however.

HIGH SCHOOL FOR BOYS

Report Form
1933
Name: L. Hughes
Remove

July 28th

Form

Times Absent 2	Age 12.11		No. in Form 30	
Times Late 0	Average Age of Form 12.9		*Position in Form 8*	
SUBJECT	**NO. IN FORM**	**POSITION**	**REMARKS**	
SCRIPTURE	29	5	Good	
ENGLISH	30	6	Strong progress	GB
GEOGRAPHY	30	4	F.Good	GWA
HISTORY	30	3	Very Good	FD
LATIN				
FRENCH	30	7=	Has worked hard	ROW
ARITHMETIC	30		Tries hard	JIW
ALGEBRA				
GEOMETRY	30	16=	More effort needed	JIW
TRIGONOMETRY				
PHYSICS	30	17	Capable of doing better	EJ
CHEMISTRY				
NATURE STUDY				
ART	30	12=	Good	RS
SINGING	30	16=	Satisfactory	HCMB
MANUAL WORK	30	14=	Good	AS
PHYSICAL EXERCISES	30	9	Satisfactory	AS
GAMES			Good	AS
CONDUCT Good			Weekly Detentions: 0 times	
GENERAL CONDUCT AND PROGRESS: L. Hughes has made good progress on the whole and his conduct is satisfactory.				
Next Term begins on			**Signed** Form Master	

Figure 11.4   Report of a pupil in a small town secondary state grammar school in 1933

 Student Activity

Identifying and analysing existing documentation about your educational history

Find what written and photographic material you can from your educational past. These could be exam certificates, annual reports, school magazines, class pictures, exercise books.

(Continued)

(Continued)

Arrange them in time order and then prepare a presentation of your educational history using a sample of these artefacts.

Teaching Plans for Infants (age 5–7)

Easter Term 1951

	Week ending 12th Jan (average 8 in class)	Week ending 19th Jan (average 8)
NUMBER	2x,3x tables. s..d table to 15d	2x, 3x, s..d tables – Number bonds of 5
	Individual work from cards	Individual work from cards
	Practical shopping up to 1/-	Shopping and weighing sand
LANGUAGE	News sheet	News sheet and weather record
ACTIVITIES	Transcription from copies	Std I – Simple comprehension on picture – 'The Farmyard'
	Top Group : Exercises from 'Ability Exercises' Book I.	→ ditto
	Poetry – An evening prayer	
NATURE &	Nature walk, and looking at	Story : Serial 'Teddy Bear's
OBSERVATION	a small stream.	Birthday Party'
	Simple talk on river action, depth, undercutting and flooding	Nature story with picture to show difference in animals' footprints in the snow
PHYSICAL EDUCATION	Indoors – music and movement.	→ ditto
	Short apparatus practices outdoors.	→ ditto
MUSIC	'Rag Dolls' action song	'Buttercups & Daisies'.
	Music and Movement	Music & Movement 'Rag Dolls'
HANDWORK ACTIVIITES	Free activity	Free activity with all available
	Renewing some goods for the shop	materials
		→ ditto
	Painting – free expression 'Of Nature Walk'	Some – woodwork

Figure 11.5   Planning by a teacher in a rural primary school on the English/Welsh border

Teachers' lesson planning

Other documents that can inform us of school life are the lesson plans written by teachers. Here are two examples of teacher planning. The first was a plan for two weeks' teaching written by a primary school teacher in 1951. The second is an example used by a student teacher of a week's lessons on the literacy hour in 2002. Such documents provide striking evidence of the way practice changes over time and prompt further questions to be asked concerning the whole nature of teaching and classroom life.

NATIONAL LITERACY STRATEGY TEACHING OBJECTIVES – WEEKLY PLANNER:				PRIMARY SCHOOL	
Class: 5	Yr Group (s): 5	Term: Spring – 1st half		Week Beg: 21st Jan 02	*Teacher*
	Whole class shared reading writing	Whole class phonics, spelling vocabulary and grammar	Guided group tasks (reading or writing)	Guided group tasks (reading or writing)	Independent group tasks	Plenary
Mon	Look at front cover illustration and title. What kind of information might they find? Use of question words in the title. Revise term explanation. P.8–9 – read the text and caption. Explanation text p.2–3 – use acetate and annotate.	Investigate and note features of impersonal style. Spellings – 10 words with suffix changing from full/ful.	ALS Group: Guided reading – Level 8.		Using a selection of non-fiction books look at contents pages of each book and identify whether the book is likely to contain explanations. Makes notes and list anything that supports their choice e.g. contents, structure etc.	One group to report back on activity. Return to page 2–3 using PCM 1. One large copy and A4 for pupils. What is an explanation text?
Tues	Read model text p.2–3. Discuss tone/level of formality of text. Does the author address the reader directly? Are personal opinions given? Paragraph 3 – identify verbs. Repeat verbs p.6–7.	Investigate verbs of past and present tense. Junior English p.58.	Red Group: Guided reading – Level 9.		Using one of the explanations from Lesson 1 ask the children to identify and list all the verbs in the present tense. Ask if verbs are used to explain how things happen or how things are. Ext: put verbs into sentences in present tense.	One group to report back. Are the words chosen actually verbs? If so are they in the present tense? How do we know?

(Continued)

Figure 11.6   (Continued)

Class: 5	Yr Group (s): 5	Term: Spring – 1st half		Week Beg: 21st Jan 02		*Teacher*
	Whole class shared reading writing	Whole class phonics, spelling vocabulary and grammar	Guided group tasks (reading or writing)	Guided group tasks (reading or writing)	Independent group tasks	Plenary
Wed	Read model text p.2–3. Look at connectives. Discuss how explanations are linked e.g. because, so. P.5 – read first sentence. Look at a how a complex sentence can be made into two shorter sentences. Repeat with para. Mammals on land.	Pronouns. Junior English p.21.	Blue Group 2: Guided reading – Level 10.		Ask children to identify and list further cause and effect connectives in other explanation texts. Using PCM 2 pupils to practise combining sentences.	Add connectives children have found to the list and discuss the appropriate use of commas. Use PCM 2.
Thurs	Mask captions on p.10 and 11. Read p.11 – the inner ear. Discuss with the children how they think an ear works. What helps their explanations and under-standings? Ask children.	Joining sentences. Junior English p.31.	Yellow Group 2: Guided reading – Level 10.	Blue Group 1: Guided reading – Level 10.	Using prepared books with masked captions ask the children to work in pairs to examine illustrations, diagrams and photographs and write captions for them.	Ask some pupils to read out their own captions before revealing the real caption. Ensure others provide comment.
Fri	**Sports Link Taster Day.**				**Sports Link Taster Day.**	

Figure 11.6   An example of a student teacher's planning for one week of literacy hour lessons
Source: Liverpool JMU

What do these documents tell us or rather what questions do they prompt?

- Is the planning of 1951 so cursory as to be worthless, or is the teacher so experienced that she does not need more than these minor prompts (a journey back in time to see this planning in action would be most instructive)?
- Does planning a whole week's literacy hour lessons allow sufficient flexibility for pupils to make differential progress each day?
- To what extent does each planning sheet facilitate differentiation?
- How is planning in either case related to assessment?
- What do these examples tell us about the relative autonomy of the teachers in terms of the curriculum?
- How slavishly do lessons follow teacher planning documents in practice?

 Student Activity

Comparing what organisations say about themselves

Choose two educational institutions of the same type e.g. two universities, two secondary schools, or two further education colleges.

Identify five important aspects of these organisations to compare, such as celebration of pupil/student success, client support, communicating information.

Search the web sites of the chosen institutions comparing how well they do on each of these five aspects.

Write a summary of your findings with a paragraph for each aspect.

Analysis of teaching texts

Thus far we have considered written documents used in educational institutions; it is also important to consider the texts that are used in the teaching process. It is these texts that make up a significant part of the curriculum that pupils receive at school. These carry messages, sometimes intended and sometimes not, that children will take with them from the classroom. It is interesting to consider the content of school texts and how they create images of what is officially important in history, geography, citizenship, and so on.

In the 1980s there was much interest in the gender and racial stereotyping portrayed in the texts and reading books used in schools. As a result of having developed equal opportunities policies, schools and LEAs began to monitor the published material that was used by their pupils. Useful research tools were developed by, for example, Genderwatch, for practitioners to use. The following examples were tools for analysing the content of books used in the classroom (see Figures 11.7 and 11.8).

Name of school ....
Filled in by .... Date completed ....

F   M   (please tick)

- Are the authors, contributors and editors, men or women? _____
- How many men and women are named in the CONTENTS list? _____
- How many men and women are in the INDEX? _____
- How many times are women mentioned in the TEXT? _____
- Do they appear as independent people or as DEPENDENTS on men (wives, etc.)?
- Are they shown in a wide range of activities or limited to STEREOTYPED ACTIVITIES (housewives, spinning, social reformers)?
- Are they described in the same way as men or is APPEARANCE emphasised?
- How many ILLUSTRATIONS include: women? _____ men? _____
- How many illustrations are there of specific women and men?_____
- Does LANGUAGE exclude stereotypical descriptions of women e.g. man, workman, farmer and wife? _____
- Does the SUBJECT MATTER, e.g. in history, emphasize and value concerns traditionally associated with men, e.g. war, diplomacy, trade, parliament, inventions, rather than concerns traditionally associated with women, e.g. family life, work, housing local politics, living standards? _____

Figure 11.7   Checklist for assessing sex bias in non-fiction books for older pupils (designed by Carol Adams, in Myers, 1992, Genderwatch)

This type of proforma proved very useful, as it could either be used as it was or easily modified as required. What such research provided for those schools that undertook it was data that enabled them to analyse their current literature provision. This formed the basis of staff discussion from which future policy could be developed and suitably monitored. Though the examples shown relate to gender they could be easily adapted to capture data relating to ethnicity, religion and other socio-cultural issues. Although originally designed for analysing books, the same methodology could be employed in the assessment of other curriculum and display material used throughout schools.

Example of an analysis of text books

We now consider a more recent study (See Hodkinson, 2007) by an Education Studies lecturer who had an interest in the government's policy on the inclusion of children with special needs into mainstream schools. The researcher, Dr Alan Hodkinson, was particularly interested in the influence of current government inclusion policy initiatives and how these were impacting upon educational practice within local schools. He first completed a literature review of recent government policy which made plain that the policy of inclusion should observe the creation of learning environments where stereotypical views were challenged and where pupils learnt to appreciate, and view positively, the differences in others, whether these differences arose from race, gender, or disability. Hodkinson wanted to ascertain whether the school textbooks commonly used by pupils in two primary schools did indeed promote the type of inclusive learning environments that the government was aiming to create.

Name of school ....
Filled in by.. Date completed ....
How many pictures are there of women/girls in your book? _____
How many pictures are there of men/boys in your book? _____
List the activities the people illustrated are doing
Women/Girls _____
Men/Boys _____
Are there differences between the types of activities women/girls are shown doing compared with those that men/boys are doing? Explain _____
_____

Figure 11.8   Checklist for assessing sex bias in non-fiction books for younger pupils (Myers, 1992, Genderwatch)

Title of the research

The cultural representation of disability and disabled people within the English education system: a critical examination of the influence of primary school textbooks

Aims

This research examined the scope of the representation and treatment of disability and disabled people within the textbooks commonly used with primary-aged pupils. The overall aim of the research was to explore whether textbooks consciously or unconsciously promoted or represented prejudices or stereotypical ideas in respects of disability or disabled people.

Method

The aim of the research meant that interview, observation and questionnaire data collection methods did not have fitness for purposes because the researcher did not want to observe how teachers employed textbooks but rather wanted to ascertain what picture of disability they contained. Thus the researcher adopted a method described as proto-text analysis. This involves observing the content and analysing the text and discourse simultaneously to uncover the explicit and implicit messages of disability conveyed within textbooks.

Sample

Two schools of a similar size and demographic make up, in a city in the North-West of England, were chosen to be the site for the data collection. The head teachers of both schools were initially contacted by letter and a follow-up phone call discussed the purpose of the research and the researcher's requirements in terms of the material that would be needed for the purposes of data collection. Each school was visited twice and during these visits the textbooks employed by teachers with years 1 to 6 pupils became the subject of analysis. This study of the representation of disability was based upon a sample of 96 textbooks published between 1974 and

2005, with the vast majority of the sample being published from the 1990s onwards. The textbooks covered six subject areas: literacy, numeracy and science, as well as personal social and health education, religious education and geography. In total, 3717 pages were subject to proto-text analysis.

Outline of the research process

1. Checklist designed for assessing the representation of people with disabilities within school textbooks (see Figure 11.9).
2. Two schools contacted and supplied with participation information sheets and ethics forms completed.
3. Research conducted and 96 books reviewed:

    (a) **Phase one** – the macro analysis involved each textbook being read page by page with any sections which referenced disability or disabled people being marked.

    (b) **Phase two** – the microanalysis stage, where the marked sections of text were examined using linguistic analysis. Here the linguistic forms within the text (such as the lexicon, agency and action, voice, verbs and adjectives) were analysed to reveal any hidden assumptions about disability and disabled people. During this phase a frequency and space analysis was also conducted; simple counting and calculating of the discrete sections of text examined how frequently disability or disabled people were mentioned.

    (c) **Phase 3** – an examination of the images, within the textbooks, was undertaken. This involved a simple tallying of the people (categorised by race, disability and gender) who were represented in each of the images.

Analysis of data

Having completed the research Hodkinson had gathered a large amount of data that related to the 'picture' of disability employed within the textbooks. To make sense of the data he employed simple statistical methods to analyse the mean amount of words in relation to disability and the number of people with disabilities pictured in each textbook. The results of the data collection were represented in graphical form (an example is given in Figure 11.10). Specific examples of text from individual textbooks were used to denote how the description of disability offered in the sample books did not match with that of the inclusive learning environment promoted by the government.

Commentary

This research example provides us with a very different approach which, though quite technical in terms of its data collection and analysis methods, is applicable to a host of possible investigations. It is also a fairly accessible approach in that students can often gain access to textbooks more easily than to pupils and teachers. A development of this study might be to consider the issue of pupil voice or teacher voice to explore the levels of engagement with the issue of how disability is represented or discussed within texts.

1. Book information

Title of book _____	Publisher _____
Year of publishing _____	No. of Pages _____
Year/Age _____	Author _____
Place of publishing _____	Subject _____

2. Illustrations/pictures

No. of illustrations _____
No. of illustrations of men_____
No. of illustrations women _____
No. of illustrations children (CH) _____
No. of illustrations race/ethnicity M __ W __CH__
No. of illustrations disability M __ __W __CH____
No of photographs disability M __ __W ___CH____

No. of photographs _____
No. of photographs men _____
No. of photographs women _____
No. of photographs children (CH) _____
No. of photographs race M __ W __

3. Description of illustrations/photographs

Comment upon: Where is the picture positioned in the text? Is it black and white or colour? What is happening in the picture? Where is the picture located i.e. school playground, etc?

4. Story line/text line

Comment upon bia – standards for success – role of disability in storyline – relationships between people – who is the hero/heroine/stereotype? Effects on self-image – disability shown as physical – every individual portrayed with unique strengths, weaknesses, interest, lifestyles. Language used in relationship to character.

Figure 11.9   Textbook Data Collection Sheet

Student Activity

Researching disability issues

In discussing Hodkinson's (2007) research we have presented only a small piece of the data analysis.

You can access his article to read the full project results, but in the meantime try to think about the range of aspects of the data that could be explored in more detail and how they might be analysed and presented.

- What are the ethical issues involved?
- How might disabled people feel about being the focus of the research?
- Does it single them out in a way that is inappropriate, or does it highlight the fact that society needs to be alert to their inclusion in mainstream thinking within education?

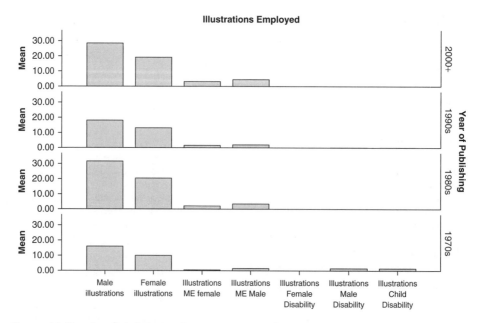

Figure 11.10   Results of data collection

Photographs and their use in research

Traditionally, academic work and the research upon which it is based has usually been presented in written form. It may have been that this was the only appropriate manner in which to transmit such material. However if, as the adage goes, a picture can paint a thousand words, then the importance of using photographic evidence in classroom-based research must also be considered. Bartlett and Burton (2007) have discussed the power of photographic evidence in depicting school organisation and teaching style in nineteenth-century schools. The starkness of huge rooms with pupils in serried rows and the 'master' on a raised dais with cane in hand needs little textual elaboration. The photographs required may have already been taken for other purposes in the past and available for use by researchers. In other instances researchers may wish to take photographs as part of the research.

As described in the case study of the evaluation of a day visit to a working farm (see Chapter 6), using photographs can be very helpful in showing a range of activities and situations and can present an immediate image that might be difficult to explain in words in the same way. However, taking and storing photographs has a particular sensitivity today that researchers need to be aware of and, as a result of this, ethics committees will need certain assurances before they allow data to be collected via photography. This is to do with the way electronic images can be made widely available and the uses to which they can be put. Images of children can be particularly problematic.

Obviously pictures taken in any research in this area are likely to be of educational activities and so should, by and large, be unproblematic. As a researcher hoping to use photographs you will need to be clear about:

- why they are being used;
- what will be photographed, i.e. how any adults and children will be portrayed;
- who will have access to them;
- what will happen to the photographs after the research has been completed;
- whether any images will be used in academic displays or publications;
- how general consent will be obtained;
- what right any individual photographed will have over the use of their images.

Very often schools and nurseries, and also colleges and universities, will have guidelines, policies and agreements on the taking of photographs. Parents and pupils are usually happy to give you consent if the reason is explained and if they can see the pictures you take. Photographs and video evidence can often support an explanation and also provide an illustration of what has been observed by you or discussed in interviews. As with all methods of data collection you will need to use photographic evidence as appropriate to your study. Whilst considering visual evidence presented in photographs and video, it is important to remain aware of the 'snapshot' nature of such images and how the particular content has been framed at the expense of something else.

There follows an example of the use of photographs and video as data in a PhD research project. The researcher here was aiming to use the digital images not just as data that she could collect, but also to enable the young children in the study to become involved themselves in deciding the visual representation that they wanted.

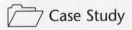 Case Study

Children's perspectives on the planning of Early Years' education and care

Angeliki was conducting an exploration into how young children understand and depict their experiences of nursery school. Her aim was to develop an understanding of how these young children perceived the curriculum of their nursery. Thus it was important to her that the children were able to be involved in all stages of the research and had some influence over what data they wanted, or did not want, to be collected. Ten children in a class at one day care centre, aged two to three years old, were the main respondents.

(Continued)

(Continued)

The researcher spent several days per week before the commencement of the research becoming acquainted with the children and the setting and allowing them to get to know her. The actual research took place over five months, mornings only, for three days per week. Before the study could be conducted Angeliki explained what would be done and why to the teachers and other adults working at the nursery, to the parents, and in an appropriate storybook form to the children. She explained how the visual images would be taken, how they would be used in the research and what would happen to them afterwards. Consent was obtained from all the adults groups and the relevant consent forms were signed. Angeliki also devised a consent form for the children at the end of their booklet that they could mark or stamp to show their consent to taking part.

Data were collected by video camera. There were two cameras with one fixed to show the nursery area. This was used to record activity in the nursery for half an hour every day. The second was used when required by the researcher and at the request of the children. A digital camera was available at all times for photographs to be taken by the researcher and also by the children if they wished. The children were also able to take voice recordings where they described activities and 'interviewed' other children about what they had done. Angeliki also made field notes and kept a personal diary of nursery activities and the children's responses that she completed every day. A daily diary was also constructed by the children, aided by staff at the nursery, as part of their regular activities.

All videos were played back to the children at the end of every morning. Recordings and photographs were also played and shown every week for the children to approve/check/pass comment. In addition Angeliki interviewed the children, parents and teachers as part of the research. The visual material helped with these interviews as it showed particular activities to talk about, refer to and discuss.

This is a fascinating research study, not least because of the age of the respondents and what it tells us about how expectations of children frame their progress. In terms of the intentions of the research, we can see how the blending of methods and the triangulation of perspectives will serve to produce a very thick descriptive account of the children's understanding of their learning experiences. A similar piece of research by Jeff Serf was outlined in Chapter 7. He used a TV advert for soap powder as stimulus to begin conversations and interviews. This work by both Jeff and Angeliki highlights how people can use both visual and verbal data to construct their worlds and how as researchers we inevitably do the same.

In summary it is helpful to remind ourselves of the advantages and disadvantages of using extant documentation.

Advantages of using extant documents

1. They help provide official versions of how different education institutions, curricula and assessment are operating at a particular point in time.
2. They demonstrate changes over time.
3. They often generate further questioning by the researcher.
4. They are a useful stimulant for further discussion by those involved.
5. They provide recorded data that may have been forgotten or not known by research participants.

Disadvantages of using extant documents

1. Written accounts may not be an accurate reflection of events as they can reflect the view or wishes of the compilers and may have been rendered politically correct.
2. The documents alone do not show how they were interpreted and used, so triangulation via other data sources beyond the documents themselves is advisable.

Conclusion

All documentary material, whether its source is a government document store or database, a publisher, the school management team, teachers, or even pupils themselves, can provide an insight into life in educational institutions and the process and outcomes of education. Such material can enhance or be enhanced by data gathered via various other research methods, such as interviews, observations and questionnaires. Documentation may provide a stimulus for interview or observation or it may provide useful contextual or explanatory data for something a researcher has found through questionnaires, observations, and so on.

Recommended Reading

Prior, L. (2003) *Using Documents in Social Research*. London: Sage. The forms, compilation and social significance of documents are discussed and the author considers the role of such documents in research. Though not specifically written for education researchers, the text is applicable for users across a range of subject areas.

12

Writing up and final conclusions

This chapter takes you through the writing up of research projects. These can be of various lengths and range from a small-scale piece of research for one module assignment to a full dissertation. Invariably all students in higher education will be involved in research in many different ways during their studies. Research findings from a range of sources are used throughout undergraduate and post-graduate studies. It is vital that you have an understanding of the research process so that you are able to use evidence appropriately.

Key points in writing up research projects and the construction of research dissertations

There are certain things that you need to make clear when writing up your research project and these can be dealt with under a number of headings. Obviously the number of words you write under each will depend upon the size of the project and the written piece you are producing. Remember that these are guidelines and it is important that you use and adapt them according to your specific research project.

1. Abstract

- *What are abstracts?* Articles in journals, research papers and dissertation theses usually have an abstract before the beginning. The length of the abstract needed is invariably laid down by the publishers or the thesis submission requirements. Depending upon the size of the whole publication they are usually expected to be between 100 and 500 words.
- *Why are they done?* Abstracts are concise accounts that summarise the whole thesis or article. The reader should be able to read the abstract and

understand the purpose and content of the article/thesis. This will enable them to decide whether the article is about what they are looking for or not. Thus good abstracts are vital for anyone conducting their literature review.

- *What should be included?* Each abstract should outline the purpose of the paper. It will say what will be looked at, why and how. It will also summarise the main conclusions. Many researchers will choose to write the final abstract after they have written their paper, though it is useful to have a rough draft at the beginning of the process that can act as a kind of plan.

 Student Activity

Constructing an abstract

- Choose a project you are currently working on.
- Choose a conference or research journal – look at the abstract requirements (i.e. word length and key contents).
- Write an abstract for it – consider the purpose, what, why, how, and your conclusions.
- Share this with other students or co-workers.

---

2. Focus, research questions and title

We dealt with these in the early chapters so you should now be aware of their importance. You must spend some time discussing your research focus. Don't assume the reason you are studying something is clear to everyone else. This discussion sets the scene for the reader and introduces them to your research. It enables you to identify the important issues and some of the main theoretical positions. You need to say why this particular focus is of interest to you. This will enable you to move on to the research questions that come out of this.

Though you may not decide on your actual title until you have nearly completed your research project, you must ensure that you give it careful consideration before you complete your final draft. The title is the first thing that anyone who comes to your project will see. Therefore it needs to give them a clear understanding of what they are about to read. Misleading or unclear titles can be very annoying for readers. A good title, on the other hand, will give the reader a clear understanding of your research and will encourage them to carry on.

3. Literature review

The purposes of the literature review are clearly stated in Chapter 5. This is a very important part of any research project as you will need to examine what has been written and researched in the area in order to place your own contribution. Chapter 5 explains how to compile and write your literature review.

4. Research design, sample and methods used to gather data

An account of how you gathered and compiled the data will be a very important part of your writing up of any research. Remember, this is not something to be hidden or skipped over. You will need to explain clearly how all the data were collected. This must include your initial 'groundwork' when you were formulating your research plan. When talking to students who have conducted research it is quite striking how often they will talk of the importance of initial conversations in helping them to decide on the types of appropriate data collection and who it would be useful to include as respondents in their research, yet none of this will be mentioned in the final account. Make sure you don't replicate this omission.

For each of the main methods of data collection that we have outlined in this book we have designed a brief *aide memoire* as to the important points that should be included in your account of the methodology. For each method you have used to collect data you will need to explain why you chose to use it. Conversely you may mention why you didn't choose particular alternative methods, which to others may have seemed more appropriate. This will show how you came to a decision about what you saw as significant and collectable data.

You will need to explain who the respondents were, how many were involved, how they were chosen, and their consent gained. You will also need to explain the design of each instrument and how the data were collected. This should include such details as where interviews were conducted, how long they took, and the structure of the interviews. For observations you will need to show clearly the number of observations that took place, the duration of each, and the particular environment in which the observation took place. For both of these methods how you recorded the data is particularly important to outline. For questionnaires you will need to ensure that you explain how the questionnaires were distributed and then collected in. Your response rate is particularly significant to mention here.

It is also important to say for each method 'how it went', discussing what you found to be the positives and negatives in using them. Whilst you should use literature to support your choice of methods in your written account, it is vital that you apply these to your own methods rather than just give generic lists of advantages and disadvantages of particular method types. Remember to include blank copies of any data collection instruments, such as questionnaires, interview and observation schedules, and log guidelines in your appendix.

You will need to show how you have addressed any ethical considerations arising from your research. This involves making clear your position and actions on informed consent, confidentiality and ensuring your research would not cause undue harm to the participants. You may also have to declare legal clearance to conduct such research if it involves certain groups. You will need to state that ethical approval has been obtained from the appropriate research ethics committee if required. This is usually a very short section but is nonetheless very important.

5. Analysis of findings

This section is very important and varies enormously from research study to research study. The factors that can shape how the data and analysis are presented will depend upon your positioning, the size of the research project and also the type of data you collected. Clearly, how you present data that consists of large amounts of statistics is likely to be very different from the presentation of a small number of in-depth interviews. One convenient way to present data and to analyse it is to concentrate on the research questions and to go through each one showing what you have found that enables you to answer these.

If you are using charts, graphs and tables of statistics try to ensure that these are clearly labelled and that they have a purpose for being there. They must not be included just to fill a space or to look impressive. Think carefully about overuse of charts. For instance, it is pointless to show bar charts for large numbers of questions having just yes/no answers. They will only show two columns each, one for 'yes' and one for 'no'. It would be far better to just write the answers in numbers or percentages than to attempt to graphically display them as pie or bar charts. Don't assume that your reader will understand why charts and tables are there. Their attention will be drawn to them when they are referred to in the surrounding text.

How you present qualitative data will also depend upon the data collected and your judgement concerning how much you use in the actual textual account. You need to show how the data you have collected can answer the research questions. You will then have to decide how to produce this. You may wish to give an overview, citing examples, quotes, and estimations of feeling. This produces what is termed 'thick descriptive analysis'.

Both of these forms of data presentation and analysis have their strengths and weaknesses. Charts, graphs and tables when well presented and used in the analysis can appear to be very impressive and authoritative. Certainly statistics do give a veneer of scientific accuracy. Detailed written accounts, on the other hand, can communicate to the reader a rich understanding of the focus and outcomes of the research. They can appear very 'human', portraying emotions such as conflict, loyalty, fear, involvement, and so on as displayed by the respondents. You will need to be sure which is appropriate for your study and able to justify your choice of presentation.

6. Conclusions

All research studies, whether presented as dissertations, reports or articles, should present some final conclusions which will draw the relationships between the original research question/s, the literature reviewed, and the findings analysed.

Example of how a research study can be written up

To illustrate how to present research we now include a précis of a research article and its construction which was based on research by Denise Barrett-Baxendale, one of our professional doctorate students, which culminated in a co-written article submitted to a school leadership journal (Barrett-Baxendale and Burton, 2009). Her research formed the first part of her professional doctorate in education studies.

1. Abstract

The following is the exact abstract that appeared in the article. Following reviewers' comments a few cosmetic changes were made to tighten it up a little.

In recent years the UK secondary educational landscape has witnessed significant change, with the introduction of an ever-extending spectrum of competing government initiatives and policies. This has resulted in the steady erosion of the traditionally recognised role of head teacher. This paper presents the results of a practitioner-based study centred on the unique professional journey of a selected group of senior incumbent head teachers from across Liverpool, United Kingdom. The purpose of the research was to consider the development of the head teacher role over a thirty-year period from 1977 to date. Five heads were interviewed about how they rose to headship and the influences and events which guided their career choices.

   Findings include acknowledgement of the requirement for self-directed career development, paucity of skills in preparation for headship, transformation in leadership models and the changing skills, qualities and qualifications required of contemporary and emergent head teachers.

2. Focus, research questions and title: 21st century head teacher – pedagogue, visionary leader or both?

The introduction explained that Denise Barrett-Baxendale, chief executive of a Liverpool trust schools' partnership, conducted research into the traditional roles of secondary school heads and the impact of policy changes on their experiences of leading schools. It also included some background information about the study.

Denise's experience told her that competing government initiatives and policies within the UK's secondary educational landscape had led to significant and unrelenting change which she contended had resulted in the gradual attrition of the traditional role of the head teacher. She characterised the traditional head as a strong, time-served disciplinarian, a teacher-practitioner, rewarded for outstanding performance within the classroom and who was focused on sound pedagogic practice. Head teachers were recognised and rewarded for being exceptional teacher-practitioners, as the very title 'head teacher' implies. It was imperative that the head teacher had the skills, qualities and qualifications to communicate effectively at all levels with a number of stakeholders to ensure the smooth and efficient operation of the school. The core educational stakeholders that the head teacher had responsibility both for and to during this period consisted of teachers, pupils, parents,

Local Education Authority officials and, in faith-based schools, the appropriate religious body. The head teacher concentrated principally upon teaching and learning, liaising with Local Education Authority officials to deliver an educational entitlement in *loco parentis*.

Thus Denise decided to study the transformation of the role and responsibilities of the traditional head teacher in England, tracking its development over a thirty-year period from 1977 to date. She was particularly interested in the unique professional journeys experienced by a representative selection of serving head teachers, as they rose to headship. This was the first phase of an ongoing analysis of the contemporary requirements of the twenty-first century school leader/manager, compared to the traditional role of head teacher.

3. Literature review

The literature review in Barrett-Baxendale and Burton (2009) asserts that there is no single universal leadership experience. Whilst not of itself controversial, it was important to consider this contention in relation to the findings of other studies so reference was made to relevant literature. Thus:

It is clear that there is no single universal leadership experience: there is a multiplicity of leadership experiences unique to each participant and setting, a view confirmed by Southworth (2006). Notwithstanding this, it is proposed that it is possible to articulate an analysis of the traditional model of headship and juxtapose that with twenty-first century leadership in the contemporary climate, considering how existing and emerging school leaders/managers will meet headship demands, whilst tackling the challenges of whole school reform.

Literature was accessed which explained the contextual and historical legacy issues within the current secondary educational arena, showing, for instance, that:

School leaders/managers are presented with a mandatory requirement to deliver a growing number of government policies and agendas (Hoyle and Wallace, 2005), more often than not competing or conflicting (Bush and Bell, 2002). The leadership models that currently exist within the secondary sector were found to be associated with an increase in statistical reporting on performance targets via the introduction of government published school league tables, against which perceptions of academic success appear to be judged. Meanwhile, a 'well-being' agenda (*Every Child Matters*, DfES, 2004) promotes and challenges schools to adopt a 'wrap-around', holistic approach to the personal achievement and improvement of life chances for their students (Smith, 2007). This agenda has required a transformation in how school leaders/managers develop and deliver their school improvement plans and relies heavily on collaboration and multi-agency target-setting, supported by a common assessment framework.

The balanced reporting of relevant literature was thus used to support the reasons for conducting the research and to crystallise its focus.

Denise's concern thus focused essentially on the complexities of contemporary leadership with its requirement to forge links between current national educational policy initiatives (for example, 'Building Schools for the Future',[1] 'Every Child Matters',[2] 'Full Service Extended Schools',[3] etc.) whilst satisfying key governmental performance indicators as measures of academic success. She maintained that, despite the raft of current reforms and developments, it is likely that the foremost commitment of school leaders is to children's learning and wanted to find out whether the expectations placed upon them conflicted with the very ethos which drives them, wherein traditional leadership models constitute their fundamental frame of reference or 'positioning' (*see Chapter 2 for a discussion of this*).

Literature reviews often need to make reference to the local setting of the research so for this Denise referred to relevant local authority data documentation.

It was anticipated that the selection of a local study would yield significant results due to the socio-economic characteristics of the city of Liverpool, ranked in the Index of Multiple Deprivation (IMD, 2004) as second highest in the country for unemployment and income deprivation. Liverpool thus provides a fertile ground for analysis since many of the recent government policy provisions are targeted directly toward tackling the issues presented by multiple social disadvantage.

Some contextual detail about Liverpool was provided, concluding with the statement that:

Despite a significant amount of inward EU investment, with urban regeneration a primary objective, the socio-economic backgrounds of many students, suffering the impact of multiple deprivations over a period of many generations, meant that a number of Liverpool schools were still failing to meet the achievement targets set down by the government.

It was then necessary to link the Liverpool context with the national policy agenda and to state clearly why it was an appropriate research setting.

One of the many positive educational developments for Liverpool had been its success in securing £400 million as part of the government's Wave Two 'Building Schools for the Future' programme. This £45 billion capital project is estimated to last fifteen years, during which time the government intends to rebuild or renew all 3,500 state secondary schools in England. For Liverpool, this represents five schools being entirely rebuilt, six schools being extensively refurbished and an additional twenty schools benefiting from a comprehensive building programme. An interesting aspect of this extensive initiative is that even the most senior and experienced incumbent head teachers have limited, if any, experience of such a vast capital development programme. Previous government spending on such a large scale preceded the appointment of even those with in excess of

---

[1] UK Government capital school redevelopment programme.
[2] Government programme for a national framework to support multi-agency collaboration across Children's Services.
[3] To provide access to a range of opportunities and services for all children beyond the school day.

thirty years' experience in the profession. Earley and Weindling (2004) confirm that head teachers have received little or no training in what are specialised fields, such as planning, accountancy, architecture and change/systems management, in preparation for the requirements placed upon them as learning architects for the twenty first century. Thus Liverpool represents an interesting case study, not least because of the range of national initiatives, implemented locally, had afforded the opportunity to develop a range of innovative intervention programmes supplementary to that offered within a traditional secondary school model. Examples of such intervention strategies include 'Full Service Extended Schools', 'City Learning Centres',[4] and 'City Academies'.[5] Although many of these locally based initiatives attract significant funding which head teachers could access to raise attainment, they also add an additional complexity to school leadership, presenting a diverse and dynamic practitioner landscape which head teachers must negotiate, a view reinforced by Salt (2007).

4. Research design, sample and methods used to gather data
The research design, sample and data gathering method chosen were described and justified, with the problems encountered also briefly outlined.

Semi-structured interviews were conducted with five senior, long-serving head teachers from across the south and east central areas of Liverpool thus the data collected were qualitative and were written up as professional narratives provided by research participants. The use of interviews was determined upon because of the desire to produce 'thick' data (Gomm and Hammersley, 2001). Seven interviews were conducted as part of the research sample – one being for pilot purposes – however, the voice recording of one of the remaining six interviews was irretrievably damaged as a result of a malfunction of the recording device. These interviews track the unique professional journey through which each research subject rose to headship.

Each research subject was presented with 12 questions, providing subjects with the flexibility to extend and/or redirect responses, dependent upon their own personal experience. Semi-structured interviews were utilised, although all research subjects were presented with the same questions to ensure a consistent approach (Burton and Bartlett, 2005). The questions, acting merely as prompts, encouraged subjects to speak freely and openly about their unique professional journey. Interview questions focused on a number of issues, including the appointment process, organisation structure and culture, and a reflective analysis of the subjects' experiences of previous head teachers' leadership styles. The question design and structure facilitated the tracking of major events, influences and changes, which had significantly contributed to the subjects' professional development and how such events had informed the manner in which they conducted the role of head teacher in a contemporary climate.

All interviews were recorded with the permission of participants and then transcribed verbatim, with subjects having the opportunity to review

---

[4]State-of-the-art learning centres offering ICT-related intervention programmes across partnerships of schools.

[5]State funded independently managed schools located in areas of high deprivation.

their transcripts. This was essential, not only to ensure the accuracy of the transcripts, but also as an integral part of any ethically sound research validation process (Burton and Bartlett, 2005).

The research sample was intentionally limited to a local study to facilitate high quality, in-depth interviews allowing the exploration of narratives that would not have been possible had the numbers been extended. Research participants were selected specifically to provide a diverse cross-section of the current head teacher community whilst at the same time being representative of the routes into headship, permitting the identification of similarities, divergences and emerging themes. Participants included:

- A longstanding head teacher, who has remained in post at the same establishment since securing head teacher status and currently runs a large, successful, specialist-status school.
- A long-serving female head teacher in a single-sex faith school (also with specialist-status) in an affluent area of the city.
- A recently appointed (three years at time of writing) head teacher of a specialist school with a very diverse cultural intake in an area of extreme deprivation.
- A longstanding practitioner with experience of leading three different schools (both comprehensive and specialist-status) as head teacher.
- A longstanding head teacher with multi-dimensional experience of school leadership from a number of perspectives, including Local Authority, Trade Union and international schools.

5. Analysis of findings

Denise analysed the interview transcripts in depth, looking for both points of similarity and uniqueness. In writing up her work for publication she and her supervisor agreed to organise the responses into three themes that they seemed to fall into naturally.

The responses fell naturally into three themes: early career experiences and influences; professional development; and contemporary expectations. The chronological career emphasis of the questions had clearly resonated with respondents as they reflected upon their leadership journeys, providing them with an organising vehicle for their experiences. Participants' reflections on personal experience revealed a paucity of sophisticated managerial skills in former head teachers. However, there was recognition of the positional power of the head teacher *per se*. One clear finding from the research was the absence of preparatory training for headship, with no clear career path, training or guidance along their journeys. Despite this, or perhaps as a direct result of it, participants displayed a strong personal motivation and resourcefulness in seeking out and securing opportunities for personal and professional development and progress. An interesting finding was the importance attributed to competencies over academic qualifications. Although there was an obvious recognition of the need for candidates to be appropriately qualified, greater emphasis was placed on communication skills, drive, passion and the ability to recognise high quality teaching in others. This demonstrates an acknowledgement of the changing role of the head teacher, which requires a multi-agency, outward looking focus and increased engagement with external drivers, in addition to a concern for teaching and learning.

6. Conclusions

Denise spent some time considering the relationship between the earlier studies she had read about and how these related to her research questions and to her own findings; following discussions with her supervisor, the conclusions of the article included the following observations.

Analysis of the current leadership landscape suggests an evolution that is likely to be transformational, requiring a fundamentally revised approach to school leadership. Formerly, school leadership revolved around the effective delivery of teaching and learning. In contrast the contemporary context has Children's Services at its core. This wraparound approach to child welfare challenges the existing structures, systems and cultures. Whilst it is crucial to preserve the pedagogical nature of the traditional school leadership model, the changes require the development of a new skill set for which emerging leaders may not be adequately qualified. Fundamentally, whilst leaders may not need to be excellent pedagogical practitioners themselves, they do need to be able both to recognise and promote such excellence, as well as to provide visionary leadership within a challenging new context.

Commentary

You can access the full outcomes of this research in Baxendale and Burton (2009) if you are interested in this particular area of research. In brief, this small study elicited some very rich data which Denise was able to report within her doctoral thesis in a highly narrative form, using direct quotes from her respondents to illustrate what she deemed to be key issues for current secondary school leaders more generally. It can be argued that, despite the small sample size, this approach to reporting data is particularly powerful when set within a robust review of the literature and related research studies in order to support the extrapolation to secondary school leadership more generally. Of course, any researcher must always be very careful to choose the responses included in the report to provide balance rather than simply to support the position they hypothesised. This was something that Denise initially struggled with, because she was so passionate about her perception that the heads she worked with were regularly impeded in making the educational progress they strived for because of the continuously changing demands made on them. Part of her journey as a researcher was coming to terms with the need to stand back and be more objective even though she was so involved in the day-to-day reality she was researching. Making this step ultimately made her research all the more powerful.

Cosmetic (but very important) touches

You should now be aware of the process by which data are collected and the decisions you must make as a researcher concerning presentation and analysis. This will enable you to be more critical as a reader when looking at a range of research. This should in turn make you more careful as to how you portray your own research and findings in the knowledge that others will cast a critical eye over your final report. However, we are not quite finished yet with advice on writing up your research.

You may not see the presentation of your finished project as important in your haste to get this piece of work finished. Indeed some writers will assume that the quality of their work will speak for itself. However, try to keep in mind that although the quality of the research is, of course, the key consideration, the way your project is presented will serve to encourage or alternatively discourage a reader from actually discovering its content. You will therefore need to check certain things before you run off the final draft:

- proof read and spell-check;
- check font size and line spacing;
- make sure quotations are formatted correctly;
- check all references are cited correctly in the text;
- ascertain all the references in the text are cited correctly in the bibliography;
- cross-check that there are no citations in the bibliography that are not in the text;
- make sure your title page is filled in correctly and your abstract is complete.

 Student Activity

Designing and critically appraising a small-scale research project

This is a collation of tasks carried out in previous chapters.

- Identify a focus for a proposed research project. Justify the focus using literature as appropriate.
- Clearly state the title and research questions.
- Relate the proposed research to paradigms.
- Identify a list of appropriate literature.
- List the methods to be used, the intended respondents, and the form of the data to be obtained. This section could be taken further by designing and piloting the actual research tools.
- Identify any limitations of the proposal.

Having completed the above you should be in a position to conduct your research project.

Final conclusions

Researching can be seen as an important part of the learning process whatever stage of our education we are at. In order to maximise our understanding of the research process some of the key issues to note are that:

- There are many research methods that can be used to collect data. Even within particular method types there can be enormous variation. Researchers can be inventive, not simply staying with questionnaires, surveys or formal observation. As a researcher you can use or adapt an existing research instrument. Note that in many cases the researcher will design his/her own instrument.
- Researchers have to make decisions concerning the methodology to be used in light of the type of data they require, which are also dependent on the purposes of the research.
- Practical constraints such as time, costs, and the nature of the respondent group will be significant factors to be taken into account when designing your research. Fitness for purpose is the key criterion for deciding upon and designing a research method.
- The data collected will be a reflection of the decisions made by you and your skills as a researcher.
- Remember that Researchers will aim to be as rigorous as possible but inevitably their beliefs and assumptions will affect their research.
- Large-scale research projects are not necessarily better than small-scale projects.
- As a researcher you will need to address various ethical issues, including the confidentiality of any data collected and gaining the relevant consents.

Research is fundamental to developing our understanding of what is happening in the world around us. Students of all ages and at every level of study need to follow where their curiosity leads and to seek answers to questions in whatever way they can. Texts, such as this one, can outline some of the possible methods that can be employed but resourceful researchers will in turn find others. Dadds and Hart (2001) have shown how innovative research methodologies, such as the use of visualisation, conversation and fictional accounts as methods of enquiry and reporting, can elicit fascinating insights into aspects of education. Stepping outside of established methodologies requires both researchers and their mentors or supervisors to be brave and bold in the face of potential criticism from traditionalists. This is an excellent time to take this step.

In effect you will need to devise your own unique tools for research and not be put off by the rhetoric that can surround academic research. Research is indeed part of learning.

Recommended Reading

Clare, J. and Hamilton, H. (eds) (2003) *Writing Research: Transforming Data into Text*. London: Churchill Livingstone. This is a very engaging book that considers not only how to write research but the various approaches taken by a range of different researcher positionings.

Bibliography

Aldrich, F. and Sheppard, L. (2000) 'Graphicacy': the fourth 'R'?, *Primary Science Review*, 64: 8–11.

Aldridge, A. and Levine, K. (2001) *Surveying the Social World*. Buckingham: Open University Press.

Altrichter, H., Posch, P. and Somkeh, B. (1993) *Teachers Investigate their Work: An Introduction to the Methods of Action Research*. London: Routledge.

Anderson, G. with Arsenault, N. (1998) *Fundamentals of Educational Research*. London: Falmer.

Arksey, H. and Knight, P. (1999) *Interviewing for Social Scientists*. London: Sage.

Ball, S. (1981) *Beachside Comprehensive: A Case Study of Secondary Schooling*. Cambridge: Cambridge University Press.

Barrett-Baxendale, D. and Burton, D. (2009) '21st century headteacher – pedagogue, visionary leader or both?: A reflection on the historical perspective and critical analysis of contemporary perception and practice', *School Leadership and Management*, (forthcoming).

Bartlett, S. (2002) 'An evaluation of the work of a group of best practice researchers', *Journal of In-service Education*, 28(3): 527–540.

Bartlett, S. and Burton, D. (eds) (2003) *Education Studies: Essential Issues*. London: Sage.

Bartlett, S. and Burton, D. (2007) *Introduction to Education Studies* (second edition). London: Sage.

Bartlett, S., Burton, D. and Peim, N. (2001) *Introduction to Education Studies*. London: Paul Chapman.

Bassey, M. (1990*)* 'On the nature of research in education (Part 2)', *Research Intelligence*, 37, Summer: 39–44.

Baumfield, V., Hall, E. and Wall, K. (2008) *Action Research in the Classroom*. London: Sage.

Becker, H. (1963) *Outsiders: Studies in the Sociology of Deviance*. New York: Free.

Bell, J. (2005) *Doing Your Research Project: A Guide for First-Time Researchers in Education and Social Science* (fourth edition). Buckingham: Open University Press.

Benton, T. and Craib, I. (2001) *Philosophy of Social Science: The Philosophical Foundations of Social Thought*. Basingstoke: Palgrave.

Blaxter, L., Hughes, C. and Tight, M. (2006) *How to Research* (third edition). Maidenhead: Open University Press.

Bottery, M. and Wright, N. (1999) 'The directed profession: Teachers and the state in the third millennium'. Paper submitted at the Annual SCETT Conference. Dunchurch, November.

Bowles, S. and Gintis, H. (1976) *Schooling in Capitalist America: Educational Reform and the Contradictions of Economic Life*. London: Routledge and Kegan Paul.

British Educational Research Association (BERA) (2004) *Revised Ethical Guidelines for Educational Research*. Nottingham: BERA.

Bryant, I. (1996) 'Action research and reflective practice'. In D. Scott and R. Usher (eds), *Understanding Educational Research*. London: Routledge.

Bryman, A. (2004) *Social Research Methods* (second edition). Oxford: Oxford University press.

Burgoyne, J. (1994) 'Stakeholder analysis'. In C. Cassell and G. Symon (eds), *Qualitative Methods in Organisational Research: A Practical Guide*. London: Sage.

Burton, D. and Bartlett, S. (2002) 'The professional nature of teaching issues for Design and Teachnology teachers'. In S. Sayers, J. Morley and B. Barnes (eds), *Issues in Design and Technology Training*. London: RoutledgeFalmer.

Burton, D. and Bartlett, S. (2005) *Practitioner Research for Teachers*. London: Paul Chapman.

Bush, T. and Bell, L. (2002) *The Principles and Practice of Educational Management*. London: Paul Chapman.

Carr, W. and Kemmis, S. (1986) *Becoming Critical: Education, Knowledge and Action Research*. London: Falmer.

Carter, K. (1998) 'School effectiveness and school improvement'. In R. Halsall (ed.), *Teacher Research and School Improvement: Opening Doors from the Inside*. Buckingham: Open University Press.

Carter, K. and Halsall, R. (1998) 'Teacher research for school improvement'. In R. Halsall (ed.), *Teacher Research and School Improvement: Opening Doors from the Inside*. Buckingham: Open University Press.

Chapman, V.L. (1999) 'A woman's life remembered: Autoethnographic reflections of an adult/educator'. Paper presented at SCUTREA 29th Annual Conference, 5–7 July, University of Warwick.

Clandinin, J.D. and Connelly, M.F. (1994) 'Personal experience methods'. In N.K. Denzin and Y.S. Lincoln (eds), *The Handbook of Qualitative Research*. Newbury Park: Sage.

Clough, P. and Nutbrown, C. (2002) *A Student's Guide to Methodology*. London: Sage.

Clough, P. and Nutbrown, C. (2007) *A Student's Guide to Methodology* (second edition). London: Sage.

Cohen, L., Manion, L. and Morrison, K. (2007) *Research Methods in Education* (sixth edition). London: RoutledgeFalmer.

Corbetta, P. (2003) *Social Research: Theory, Methods and Techniques*. London: Sage.

Creemers, B. (1994) 'The history, value and purpose of school effectiveness studies'. In D. Reynolds et al. (eds), *Advances in School Effectiveness: Research and Practice*: Oxford Pergamon.

Cuff, E. and Payne, G. with Francis, D., Hustler, D. and Sharrock, W. (1984) *Perspectives in Sociology* (second edition). London: Allen and Unwin.

Dadds, M. and Hart, S. (2001) *Doing Practitioner Research Differently*. London: RoutledgeFalmer.

Deming, W. (1986) *Out of the Crisis: Quality, Productivity and Competitive Position*. Cambridge: Cambridge University Press.

Denscombe, M. (2003) *A Good Research Guide* (second edition). Maidenhead: Open University Press.

DfEE (1999) *A Fast Track for Teachers*. London: DfEE Publications Centre.

DfES (2001) *Schools Achieving Success*. London: DfES.

DfES (2004) *Every Child Matters: Change for Children*. London: DfES.

Douglas, J.W.B. (1964) *The Home and the School*. St Albans: Panther.

Drever, E. and Cope, P. (1999) 'Students' use of theory in an initial teacher education programme', *Journal of Education for Teaching*, 25(2): 97–109.

Durkheim, E. (1964) *The Rules of Sociological Method*. New York: Free.

Durkheim, E. (1970) *Suicide: A Study in Sociology*. London: Routledge and Kegan Paul.

Earley, P. and Weindling, D. (2004) *Understanding School Leadership*. London: Paul Chapman.

Edwards, R. and Usher, R. (2000) *Globalisation and Pedagogy: Space, Place and Identity*. London: Routledge.

Elliott, J. (1991) *Action Research for Educational Change.* Milton Keynes: Open University Press.

Elliott, J. (1998) *The Curriculum Experiment: Meeting the Challenge of Social Change.* Buckingham: Open University Press.

Elliott, J. (2001) 'Making evidence-based practice educational', *British Educational Research Journal*, 27(5): 555–574.

Elliott, J. (2003) Interview with John Elliott, 6 December, *Educational Action Research*, 11(2): 169–180.

Elliott, J. (2006) 'Educational research as a form of democratic rationality', *Journal of Philosophy of Education*, 40(2): 169–186.

Evans, K. and King, D. (2006) *Studying Society: The Essentials.* Oxon: Routledge.

EPPI-Centre (2003) About the EPPI-Centre. Available at: http://eppi.ioe.ac.uk/EPPIWeb/home.aspx

Flick, U. (2002) *An Introduction to Qualitative Research.* London: Sage.

Freeman, J. (1998) *Educating the Very Able: Current International Research (OfSTED Reviews of Research).* London: The Stationery Office.

Glaser, B. and Strauss, A. (1967) *The Discovery of Grounded Theory.* Chicago: Aldane.

Goffman, E. (1971) *The Presentation of Self in Everyday Life.* London: Penguin.

Gomm, R. and Hammersley, M. (2001) 'Thick ethnographic description and thin models of complexity'. Paper presented at the British Educational Research Association Annual Conference, Leeds University, 13–15 September. Education-line internet document collection at: http://www.leeds.ac.uk/educol/documents/00001820.htm

Gomm, R., Hammersley, M. and Forster, P. (eds) (2000) *Case Study Method: Key Issues, Key Texts.* London: Sage.

Hammersley, M. (2002) *Educational Research, Policymaking and Practice.* London: Paul Chapman.

Hammersley, M. (ed.) (2007) *Educational Research and Evidence Based Practice.* London: Sage and the Open University.

Hammersley, M. and Atkinson, I. (2007) *Ethnography: Principles in Practice* (third edition). London: Routledge.

Hargreaves, D. (1972) *Interpersonal Relations in Education.* London: Routledge and Kegan Paul.

Hargreaves, D. (1996) *Teaching as a Research Based Profession: Possibilities and Prospects.* The Teacher Training Agency, Annual Lecture, Birmingham.

Harris, D.L. and Anthony, H.M. (2001) 'Collegiality and its role in teacher development: perspectives from veteran and novice teachers', *Teacher Development*, 5(3): 371–389.

Heaney, S. (2001) 'Experience of induction in one local education authority', *Mentoring and Tutoring*, 9(3): 241–254.

Heikkinen, H.L.T., Huttunen, R. and Syrjala, L. (2007) 'Action research as narrative: five principles for validation', *Educational Action Research*, 15(1): 5–19.

Hillage, J., Pearson, R., Anderson, A. and Tamkin, P. (1998) *Excellence in Research on Schools.* London: Department of Education and Employment.

Hitchcock, G. and Hughes, D. (1995) *Research and the Teacher* (second edition). London: Routledge.

Hodkinson, A. (2007) 'Inclusive Education and the cultural representation of disability and disabled people within the English education system: a critical examination of the mediating influence of primary school textbooks', *IARTEM e-Journal*, 1(1). Available at: http://www.iartem.no

Hopkins, D. (2001) *School Improvement for Real.* London: RoutledgeFalmer.

Hopkins, D. (2008) *A Teacher's Guide to Classroom Research* (fourth edition). Maidenhead: Open University Press.

Hopkins, D. and Harris, A. (2000) *Creating the Conditions for Teaching and Learning.* London: David Fulton.

Hoyle, E. and Wallace, M. (2005) *Educational Leadership: Ambiguity, Professionals and Managerialism.* London: Sage.

Israel, M. and Hay, I. (2006) *Research Ethics for Social Scientists: Between Ethical Conduct and Regulation.* London: Sage.

Jensen, A.R. (1973) *Educational Differences.* London: Methuen.

Jones, K. (2003) *Education in Britain: 1944 to the Present.* Oxford: Polity.

Kemmis, S. and Wilkinson, M. (1998) 'Participatory action research and the study of practice. In B. Atweh, S. Kemmis and P. Weeks (eds), *Action Research in Practice.* London: Routledge.

Lacey, C. (1970) *Hightown Grammar: The School as a Social System.* Manchester: Manchester University Press.

Lather, P. (2004) 'Scientific research in education: a critical perspective', *British Educational Research Journal*, 30(6): 759–772.

Lawson, J. and Silver, H. (1973) *A Social History of Education in England.* London: Methuen.

Lewin, K. (1946) 'Action research and minority problems', *Journal of Social Issues*, 2: 34–36.

Lewis, I. and Munn, P. (1997) *So You Want to do Research! A Guide for Beginners on how to Formulate Research Questions.* Edinburgh: SCRE.

Long, M. (1953) 'Children's reactions to geographical pictures', *Geography*, 180.

Mackintosh, M. (1998) 'Learning from photographs'. In S. Scoffham (ed.), *Primary Sources: Research Findings in Primary Geography.* Sheffield: Geographical Association.

Mansell, W. (2001) 'Performance pay saps teacher morale', *Times Educational Supplement*, 21 September, p. 1.

Maykut, P. and Morehouse, R. (1994) *Beginning Qualitative Research.* London: Falmer.

Mcneill, P. and Chapman, S. (2005) *Research Methods* (third edition). London: Routledge.

McNiff, J. (1988) *Action Research: Principles and Practice.* London: Macmillan.

McNiff, J. with Whitehead, J. (2002) *Action Research: Principles and Practice* (second edition). London: RoutledgeFalmer.

Miles, M. and Huberman, M. (1994) *Qualitative Data Analysis.* London: Sage.

Miller, N. and West, L. (2003) 'The auto/biographical 'we': our search for a voice in academic writing'. Paper presented at SCUTREA, 33rd annual conference, University of Wales, Bangor, 1–3 July.

Montgomery, D. (1999) *Positive Teacher Appraisal Through Classroom Observation.* London: David Fulton.

Myers, K. (1992) *Genderwatch! After the Education Reform Act.* Cambridge: Cambridge University Press.

Oliver, P. (2003) *The Student's Guide to Research Ethics.* Maidenhead: Open University Press.

Oppenheim, A.N. (1966) *Questionnaire Design and Attitude Measurement.* London: Heinemann.

Piaget, J. (1932) *The Moral Judgement of the Child.* New York:

Pole, C. and Lampard, R. (2002) *Practical Social Investigation: Qualitative and Quantitative Methods in Social Research.* London: Prentice Hall.

Pring, R. (2004) *Philosophy of Educational Research* (second edition). London: Continuum.

Prior, L. (2003) *Using Documents in Social Research.* London: Sage.

Punch, K. (1998) *Introduction to Social Research: Quantitative and Qualitative Approaches.* London: Sage.

Punch, K. (2005) *Introduction to Social Research* (second edition). London: Sage.

Reynolds, D., Creemers, B., Bird, J., Farrell, S. and Swint, F. (1994) 'School effectiveness – the need for an international perspective'. In D. Reynolds, B. Creemers, P. Nesselrodt, E. Schaffer, S. Stringfield and C. Teddlie (eds), *Advances in School Effectiveness Research and Practice.* Oxford: Pergamon.

Roberts, B. (2002) *Biographical Research.* Buckingham: Open University Press.

Rutter, M., Maughan, B., Mortimore, P. and Oulston, J. (1979*) Fifteen Thousand Hours.* London: Open Books.

Salt, T. (2007) 'Time to take the lead'. *LDR Magazine,* National College for School Leadership, January.

Sammons, P., Hillman, J. and Mortimore, P. (1995) *Key Characteristics of Effective Schools: A Review of School Effectiveness Research.* London: Office for Standards in Education.

Scholtes, P. (1998) *The Leaders' Handbook: Making Things Happen, Getting Things Done.* New York: McGraw-Hill.

Sieber, J. (1992) *Planning Ethically Responsible Research: A Guide for Students and Internal Review Boards.* London: Sage.

Silverman, D. (2005) *Doing Qualitative Research* (second edition). London: Sage.

Smith, D. (2007) 'Today's practice: tomorrow's leadership', *LDR Magazine,* National College for School Leadership, January.

Southworth, G. (2006) 'A new flame', *LDR Magazine,* National College for School Leadership, January.

Stenhouse, L. (1983) *Authority, Education and Emancipation.* London: Heinemann.

Stott, K. (1994) 'Teaching Geography using photographs'. Unpublished dissertation, Canterbury Christ Church College.

Swennen, A., Volman, M. and van Essen, M. (2008) 'The development of the professional identity of two teacher educators in the context of Dutch teacher education', *European Journal of Teacher Education,* 31(2): 169–184.

Taylor, D. and Proctor, M. (2001) *The Literature Review: A Few Tips On Conducting It.* University of Toronto, available at: http://www.utoronto.ca/writing/litrev.html

Teacher Training Agency (TTA) (1996) *Teaching as a Research-based Profession.* (Prepared by the TTA and the Central Office of Information 3/96. TETR J036294JJ.) London: The Teacher Training Agency Information Section.

Teddlie, C. and Reynolds, D. (2000) *International Handbook of School Effectiveness Research.* London: Falmer.

Thompson, M. (2000) 'Performance management: new wine in old bottles', *Professional Development Today,* 3(3): 9–19.

Thrupp, M. (2001) 'Recent school effectiveness counter-critiques: problems and possibilities', *British Educational Research Journal,* 27(4): 443–458.

Tooley, J. and Darby, D. (1998) *Educational Research: A Critique.* London: OfSTED.

Turner, J. (2003) 'The origins of positivism: the contributions of August Comte and Herbert Spencer'. In G. Ritzer and B. Smart (eds), *Handbook of Social Theory.* London: Sage.

Usher, R. (1995) 'Telling the story of the self/deconstructing the self of the story'. Annual SCUTREA Conference, University of Southampton.

Verma, G. and Mallick, K. (1999) *Researching Education: Perspectives and Techniques.* London: Falmer.

Vygotsky, L.S. (1978) *Mind in Society: The Development of Higher Psychological Processes.* London: Harvard University Press.

Walford, G. (2001) *Doing Qualitative Educational Research: A Personal Guide to the Research Process.* London: Continuum.

Waterland, L. (2001) 'Not a perfect offering'. In M. Dadds and S. Hart (eds), *Doing Practitioner Research Differently.* London and New York: RoutledgeFalmer. pp. 121–139.

Wheldall, K. and Merreit, F. (1985) *The Behavioural Approach to Teaching Package.* Birmingham: Positive Products.

Whitty, G. (2006) 'Education(al) research and education policy making: is conflict inevitable?', *British Educational Research Journal,* 32(2): 159–176.

Willmott, R. (1999) 'School effectiveness research: an ideological commitment?', *Journal of Philosophy of Education,* 33(2): 253–267.

Woods, P. (2006) *Successful Writing for Qualitative Researchers* (second edition). London: Routledge.

Yates, S. (2004) *Doing Social Science Research.* London: Sage and the Open University Press.

Yin, R. (2009) Case Study Research: Design and Methods (fourth edition). Thousand Oaks, CA: Sage.

Index